Presented to:

_____

From:

_____

Date:

_____

Names to Live By

OVER 1000 MEANINGFUL

CHRISTIAN NAMES

for YOUR BABY

HONOR **HB** BOOKS

Inspiration and Motivation for the Seasons of Life

COOK COMMUNICATIONS MINISTRIES
Colorado Springs, Colorado • Paris, Ontario
KINGSWAY COMMUNICATIONS LTD
Eastbourne, England

Honor Books is an imprint of
Cook Communications Ministries, Colorado Springs, CO 80918
Cook Communications, Paris, Ontario
Kingsway Communications, Eastbourne, England

NAMES TO LIVE BY: Over 1,000 of the Best and Most Meaningful Baby Names
© 2007 Honor Books

First Printing, 2007
Printed in the United States of America

1 2 3 4 5 6 7 8 9 10

Cover Design: Zoe Tennesen Eck Design; Thinkpen Design, llc
Interior Design: Zoe Tennesen Eck Design
Interior Production: Julie Brangers
Photo and Illustration: Dex Image, Corbis, Comstock Select, Getty Images, Shutterstock, Digital Vision, Eyewire

ISBN 978-1-56292-826-1

Introduction

"What's in a name?" Shakespeare asked in *Romeo and Juliet*. But the question really started much earlier than Shakespeare. We need look no further than Abraham and Sarah in the Bible to see how changing their names meant their lives were changing too. Their new names, meaning "father of a multitude" and "princess of the multitude," demonstrated God's covenant with them.

The Bible is full of examples of people whose names seemed to determine their destinies or captured the circumstances surrounding their births. What biblical family wouldn't feel the joy of naming a baby "laughter" (Isaac) or the assurance of "the salvation of the Lord" (Isaiah)? What little girl wouldn't rise to the occasion of being named "helper" and "defender" (Alexandria) or feel the grace of being named for the palm tree (Tamar)? Names may not determine children's fate, but they do capture parents' hopes, dreams, and aspirations for their children.

Bible-time parents knew the importance of choosing the right name for their child. And now it's your turn. As a parent-to-be, you've probably tried out different names to see how they mesh with your last name. You've thought of important ancestors and relatives who would be honored by your baby carrying their names. And perhaps you have thought of the spiritual heritage and significance a name can confer on your child. You want to choose a name that sounds right, of course, but you also want to give your child a name to live by.

Names to Live By is the perfect book for you. It offers you the nearly endless possibilities of a vast array of names, and each one conveys a special meaning, a rich heritage, and a unique key Bible verse that can help guide your child through life. While there certainly are baby name books that include more names, none will guide you as a parent in quite the same way this book will.

It is our sincere prayer that *Names to Live By* is a blessing to you as you plan for the arrival of your little one. As you reflect on the meanings and significance of the names in this book, we pray that you'll find *just* the right name for your child in its pages.

"REMEMBER THAT A MAN'S NAME IS, TO
HIM, THE SWEETEST AND MOST IMPORTANT
SOUND IN ANY LANGUAGE."

— DALE CARNEGIE

A

Aarao (SEE AARON)

Aaron (M/F)

MEANING: "enlightened"

SIGNIFICANCE: Aaron of the Old Testament was the brother of Moses and Israel's first high priest.

KEY VERSE: Let your light shine before men, that they may see your good deeds and praise your Father in heaven. (Matt. 5:16)

Aaronas (SEE AARON)

Abbot (M)

MEANING: "father"

SIGNIFICANCE: An abbot is the head, or director, of a monastery.

KEY VERSE: As a father has compassion on his children, so the LORD has compassion on those who fear him. (Ps. 103:13)

Abdon (M/F)

MEANING: "servant"

SIGNIFICANCE: In the Bible, Abdon was one of the messengers sent by King Josiah to Huldah the prophetess regarding a just-discovered copy of the law of Moses.

KEY VERSE: If anyone serves, he should do it with the strength God provides. (1 Peter 4:11)

Abel (M)

MEANING: "breath"

SIGNIFICANCE: In the Bible, Abel was the second-born son of Adam and Eve who brought a pleasing offering to God and was killed by his older brother, Cain.

KEY VERSE: May the words of my mouth and the meditation of my heart be pleasing in your sight, O LORD, my Rock and my Redeemer. (Ps. 19:14)

Abelard (M)

MEANING: "noble"; "resolute"

SIGNIFICANCE: Peter Abelard (1079–1142) was a French philosopher and theologian who greatly influenced the thinkers of his time. Later in life he was criticized for giving reason too high a place in theology, which he completely denied.

KEY VERSE: Understanding is a fountain of life to those who have it. (Prov. 16:22)

Abida (M/F)

MEANING: "father of knowledge"

SIGNIFICANCE: In the Bible, Abida was a grandson of Abraham.

KEY VERSE: The heart of the discerning acquires knowledge; the ears of the wise seek it out. (Prov. 18:15)

Abiel (M/F)

MEANING: "God is the father"

SIGNIFICANCE: In the Bible, Abiel was the great-grandfather of Saul, the first king of Israel.

KEY VERSE: I will be a Father to you, and you will be my sons and daughters, says the Lord Almighty. (2 Cor. 6:18)

Abigail (F)

MEANING: "father of joy"

SIGNIFICANCE: In the Bible, Abigail's quick thinking saved her household from certain destruction when she impressed King David with her wisdom, beauty, and dignity.

KEY VERSE: We also pray that you will be strengthened with his glorious power so you will have all the patience and endurance you need. May you be filled with joy. (Col. 1:11 NLT)

Abner (M)

MEANING: "father of light"

SIGNIFICANCE: In the Bible, Abner was the commander of King Saul's army. After Saul's death, Abner eventually made peace with the new king, David. When Abner was killed, David mourned his death and gave him a funeral befitting a great leader.

KEY VERSE: Every good and perfect gift is from above, coming down from the Father of the heavenly lights, who does not change like shifting shadows. (James 1:17)

Abra (F)

MEANING: "earth mother"

SIGNIFICANCE: Saint Abra (342–60) was the daughter of Saint Hilary of Poitiers and helped spread the faith around Poitiers, France.

KEY VERSE: The earth is the LORD's, and everything in it. (Ps. 24:1)

Abraham (M)

MEANING: "father of many"

SIGNIFICANCE: Abraham is a key personality in the Bible, and the founder of the Jewish nation. He is noted for believing God "by faith."

KEY VERSE: "Abraham believed God, and it was credited to him as righteousness," and he was called God's friend. (James 2:23)

Abrahan (SEE ABRAHAM)

Abramo (SEE ABRAHAM)

Ada (F)

MEANING: "prosperous"; "happy"

SIGNIFICANCE: Saint Ada (died seventh century) was a nun at Soissons, France, and the niece of Saint Engelbert; her whole family was known for its piety.

KEY VERSE: Trust in the LORD and do good. Then you will live safely in the land and prosper. (Ps. 37:3 NLT)

Adah (M/F)

MEANING: "prosperous;" "happy"

SIGNIFICANCE: In the Bible, Adah was the father of Jubal, who has been called the father of music and is credited with having developed the first musical instruments.

KEY VERSE: Trust in the LORD and do good. Then you will live safely in the land and prosper. (Ps. 37:3 NLT)

Adam (M)

MEANING: "man from the red earth"

SIGNIFICANCE: Adam was the first man God created.

KEY VERSE: The LORD's unfailing love surrounds the man who trusts in him. (Ps. 32:10)

Adamh (SEE ADAM)

Adamo (SEE ADAM)

A

Adan (SEE ADAM)

Adao (SEE ADAM)

Addala (SEE ADELAIDE)

Addi (M/F)

MEANING: "noble"; "kind"

SIGNIFICANCE: Addi is listed in Luke's genealogy as an ancestor of Jesus.

KEY VERSE: Clothe yourselves with compassion, kindness, humility, gentleness and patience. (Col. 3:12)

Adela (F)

MEANING: "noble"

SIGNIFICANCE: Saint Adela (died 1137) was the youngest daughter of William the Conqueror. She was active in politics all her life and contributed to several churches and monasteries.

KEY VERSE: Whatever is true, whatever is noble, whatever is right, whatever is pure, whatever is lovely, whatever is admirable—if anything is excellent or praiseworthy—think about such things. (Phil. 4:8)

Adelaide (F)

MEANING: "noble"

SIGNIFICANCE: Saint Adelaide (c. 931–99) was a princess who, as an adult, used her position and wealth to help the poor, evangelize, and build and restore monasteries and churches. Later in life, she retired to the convent she had built. Though she never became a nun, she spent the rest of her days there in prayer.

KEY VERSE: Let the righteous rejoice in the LORD and take refuge in him; let all the upright in heart praise him! (Ps. 64:10)

Adele (SEE ADELAIDE)

Adelina (F)

MEANING: "noble"

SIGNIFICANCE: Granddaughter of William the Conqueror, Saint Adelina (died 1125) was abbess of the convent founded by her brother, Saint Vitalis.

KEY VERSE: The highway of the upright avoids evil; he who guards his way guards his life. (Prov. 16:17)

Adiel (M/F)

MEANING: "ornament of God"

SIGNIFICANCE: In the Bible, Adiel is named as an ancestor of Maasai, a priest of Israel who was one of the first to return to Israel after the Babylonian captivity.

KEY VERSE: [God] has made everything beautiful in its time. (Eccl. 3:11)

Adin (M/F)

MEANING: "feminine"

SIGNIFICANCE: In the Bible, Adin was a political leader who, along with several others, signed Ezra's covenant of faithfulness to God after the exile.

KEY VERSE: The word of the LORD is right and true; he is faithful in all he does. (Ps. 33:4)

Adlai (M/F)

MEANING: "my witness"

SIGNIFICANCE: In the Bible, Adlai is the name of the father of Shaphat, the shepherd for King David.

KEY VERSE: How beautiful on the mountains are the feet of those who bring good news, who proclaim peace, who bring good tidings. (Isa. 52:7)

Adrian (M/F)

MEANING: "dark"

SIGNIFICANCE: It is said that while directing the torture of a group of Christians, Saint Adrian of Nicomedia (died 304) asked them what reward they expected to receive from God. They replied by quoting 1 Corinthians 2:9: "No eye has seen, no ear has heard, no mind has conceived what God has prepared for those who love him." He was so amazed at their courage that he publicly confessed his faith. He was imprisoned, tortured, and killed the following day. Afterward, he and several other martyrs were taken to be burned. When the executioners began to burn their bodies, a thunderstorm arose and extinguished the furnace; lightning killed several of the executioners.

KEY VERSE: No eye has seen, no ear has heard, and no mind has imagined what God has prepared for those who love him. (1 Cor. 2:9 NLT)

Adriano (SEE ADRIAN)

Adriel (M/F)

MEANING: "flock of God"

SIGNIFICANCE: In the Bible, King Saul gave one of his daughters to Adriel in marriage.

KEY VERSE: I [Jesus] am the good shepherd; I know my sheep and my sheep know me. (John 10:14)

Adrien (SEE ADRIAN)

A

Adrienne (SEE ADRIAN)

Adry (SEE ADRIAN)

Affonso (SEE ALPHONSE)

Afra (M/F)

   MEANING: "peaceful ruler"

   SIGNIFICANCE: Aphra Behn (1640–89) was the first woman writer to make a living using her own name in her writing.

   KEY VERSE: I will lie down and sleep in peace, for you alone, O LORD, make me dwell in safety. (Ps. 4:8)

Agacia (SEE AGATHA)

Agafia (SEE AGATHA)

Agata (SEE AGATHA)

Agatha (M/F)

   MEANING: "good"

   SIGNIFICANCE: It is said that while Saint Agatha (died c. 250) was being tortured for her faith, God interrupted her agony with an earthquake. As she thanked him for delivering her, she passed immediately into heaven.

   KEY VERSE: Do good, O LORD, to those who are good, to those who are upright in heart. (Ps. 125:4)

Agostino (SEE AUGUSTUS)

Aharah (M/F)

   MEANING: "meadow of sweet savor"

SIGNIFICANCE: In the Bible, Aharah was a son of Benjamin, youngest son of Jacob.

KEY VERSE: Taste and see that the LORD is good. (Ps. 34:8)

Ahava (M/F)

MEANING: "water"

SIGNIFICANCE: In the Bible, the Jewish exiles met with Ezra by the banks of this river just before their return to Jerusalem.

KEY VERSE: As the deer pants for streams of water, so my soul pants for you, O God. (Ps. 42:1)

Ahira (M/F)

MEANING: "brother of the shepherd"

SIGNIFICANCE: In the Bible, Ahira was chief of the tribe of Naphtali at the time of the Exodus.

KEY VERSE: The LORD is my shepherd, I shall not be in want. He makes me lie down in green pastures, he leads me beside quiet waters. (Ps. 23:1–2)

Ahlai (F)

MEANING: "Jehovah is staying"

SIGNIFICANCE: In the Bible, Ahlai was a descendant of Judah. That her name was listed in a genealogy may indicate she was a woman of significance.

KEY VERSE: God has said, "Never will I leave you; never will I forsake you." (Heb. 13:5)

Aidan (M)

MEANING: "little fire"

A

SIGNIFICANCE: Saint Aidan (died 651), known for his knowledge of the Bible, his eloquent preaching, his personal holiness, simple life, scholarship, and charity, founded a monastery that became a great storehouse of European literature and learning during the Dark Ages.

KEY VERSE: Love flashes like fire, the brightest kind of flame. (Song 8:6 NLT)

Aimee (F)

MEANING: "beloved"

SIGNIFICANCE: Aimee Semple McPherson (1890–1944) was the flamboyant preacher and founder of the International Church of the Foursquare Gospel.

KEY VERSE: Let the beloved of the LORD rest secure in him, for he shields him all day long, and the one the LORD loves rests between his shoulders. (Deut. 33:12)

Alain (SEE ALAN)

Alan (M)

MEANING: "handsome"; "cheerful"

SIGNIFICANCE: Alan de la Roche (1428–75) was a Dominican father and a theologian famous for his sermons.

KEY VERSE: A cheerful heart is good medicine. (Prov. 17:22)

Alano (SEE ALAN)

Alanus (M)

MEANING: "rock"

SIGNIFICANCE: Alanus was the seventh-century founder and abbot of a monastery in Gascony.

KEY VERSE: My salvation and my honor depend on God; he is my mighty rock, my refuge. (Ps. 62:7)

Alastair (SEE ALEXANDER)

Alban (M)

MEANING: "fair"; "white"

SIGNIFICANCE: Saint Alban (died c. 305) was converted by a priest he sheltered from persecutions and rescued by changing clothes with him.

KEY VERSE: Those who are wise will shine like the brightness of the heavens. (Dan. 12:3)

Albert (M)

MEANING: "noble and bright"

SIGNIFICANCE: Saint Albert the Great (1206–80) was a monk known for his study of the natural sciences and was referred to as the "Universal Doctor."

KEY VERSE: The path of the righteous is like the first gleam of dawn, shining ever brighter till the full light of day. (Prov. 4:18)

Albertko (SEE ALBERT)

Alberto (SEE ALBERT)

Albertok (SEE ALBERT)

Alda (F)

MEANING: "prosperous"

SIGNIFICANCE: Saint Alda (1249–1309) was a laywoman who devoted her life to personal penance and charity to the poor.

KEY VERSE: A generous man will prosper; he who refreshes others will himself be refreshed. (Prov. 11:25)

Alec (SEE ALEXANDER)

Alecio (SEE ALEXANDER)

Alejandro (SEE ALEXANDER)

Alek (SEE ALEXANDER)

Aleksander (SEE ALEXANDER)

Aleth (F)

MEANING: "truth"

SIGNIFICANCE: Saint Aleth of Dijon (died 1105) was the mother of Saint Bernard and other holy children.

KEY VERSE: Let us not love with words or tongue but with actions and in truth. (1 John 3:18)

Alexander (M)

MEANING: "defender of men"

SIGNIFICANCE: Alexander the Great (356 BC–323 BC) was a Greek general known for conquering much of the area around the Mediterranean and establishing an empire.

KEY VERSE: A father to the fatherless, a defender of widows, is God in his holy dwelling. (Ps. 68:5)

Alexandria (F)

MEANING: "helper and defender of humankind"

SIGNIFICANCE: The ancient city of Alexandria is best known for two things: its lighthouse, one of the seven wonders of the ancient world; and its library, which was filled with the writings of such philosophers as Aristotle and Plato.

KEY VERSE: He will cover you with his feathers. He will shelter you with his wings. His faithful promises are your armor and protection. (Ps. 91:4 NLT)

Alexio (SEE ALEXANDER)

Alexis (SEE ALEXANDER)

Alfa (SEE ALPHONSE)

Alfero (SEE ALFRED)

Alfred (M)

MEANING: "wise counselor"

SIGNIFICANCE: Alfred comes from two Old English words: *aelf* [elf] and *raed* [counsel]. In mythology and fantasy, elves are typically considered good and wise.

KEY VERSE: I [God] will instruct you and teach you in the way you should go; I will counsel you and watch over you. (Ps. 32:8)

Ali (M/F)

MEANING: "placed on the highest"

SIGNIFICANCE: Muhammad Ali (born 1942) is a world-renowned boxer known for his saying, "Float like a butterfly; sting like a bee."

KEY VERSE: Be exalted, O LORD, in your strength; we will sing and praise your might. (Ps. 21:13)

Alifonzo (SEE ALPHONSE)

Allesandro (SEE ALEXANDER)

Alois (SEE LOUIS)

Aloisa (SEE LOUISE)

Alphaeus (M)

MEANING: "son of a renowned father"

SIGNIFICANCE: In the Bible, Alphaeus was the father of apostles James and Matthew.

KEY VERSE: How great is the love the Father has lavished on us, that we should be called children of God! And that is what we are! (1 John 3:1)

Alphonse (M)

MEANING: "eager for battle"

SIGNIFICANCE: Saint Alphonsus Liguori (1696–1787) was a lawyer who promised he would never waste a moment of his life, and held fast to this vow for more than ninety years.

KEY VERSE: Be strong in the Lord and in his mighty power. (Eph. 6:10)

Alphonz (SEE ALPHONSE)

Alturo (SEE ARTHUR)

Alvah (M/F)

MEANING: "sublime"

SIGNIFICANCE: In the Bible, Alvah was a descendent of Esau and a chief of Edom.

KEY VERSE: Come and see what God has done, how awesome his works in man's behalf! (Ps. 66:5)

A

Alyn (SEE ALAN)

Amada (SEE AIMEE)

Amadia (SEE AIMEE)

Amadore (SEE AIMEE)

Amalia (SEE AIMEE)

Amadeo (SEE AMADEUS)

Amadeus (M)

MEANING: "lover of God"

SIGNIFICANCE: Wolfgang Amadeus Mozart (1756–91) was one of the greatest and most significant composers of European classical music.

KEY VERSE: Love the LORD your God with all your heart and with all your soul and with all your strength. (Deut. 6:5)

Amal (SEE EMIL)

Amana (M/F)

MEANING: "perennial"

SIGNIFICANCE: In the Bible, Song of Solomon 4:8 refers to Amana as a mountain near Damascus.

KEY VERSE: Trust in the LORD forever, for the LORD, the LORD, is the Rock eternal. (Isa. 26:4)

Amand (M)

MEANING: "worthy of love"

SIGNIFICANCE: Saint Amand (c. 584–c. 679) was a father of monasticism in ancient Belgium. When he went to live in a monastery, his father threatened to disinherit him unless he came home. Amand's reply: "Christ is my only inheritance."

KEY VERSE: Let us love one another, for love comes from God. (1 John 4:7)

Amaryllis (F)

MEANING: "lily"

SIGNIFICANCE: This flower symbolizes renewal.

KEY VERSE: Those who hope in the LORD will renew their strength. They will soar on wings like eagles; they will run and not grow weary, they will walk and not be faint. (Isa. 40:31)

Ambrose (M)

MEANING: "immortal"

SIGNIFICANCE: Saint Ambrose of Milan (c. 340–397) was known as the "honey-tongued doctor" because of his gift of preaching. He valued words and said, "Let no word escape your lips in vain or be uttered without depth of meaning."

KEY VERSE: For God so loved the world that he gave his one and only Son, that whoever believes in him shall not perish but have eternal life. (John 3:16)

Amelia (F)

MEANING: "hard-working"

SIGNIFICANCE: American aviator Amelia Earhart (1897–missing 1937), in 1928, became the first woman to fly a plane across the Atlantic.

KEY VERSE: Whatever you do, work at it with all your heart, as working for the Lord, not for men. (Col. 3:23)

Amelie (SEE AMELIA)

Amelina (SEE AMELIA)

Ameline (SEE AMELIA)

Amelita (SEE AMELIA)

Amethyst (F)

MEANING: "purple"

SIGNIFICANCE: In the Bible, God commanded Moses to include an amethyst, representing one of the twelve tribes of Israel, on the breast piece of the high priest. Leonardo da Vinci wrote that amethyst was able to dispel evil thoughts and increase intelligence.

KEY VERSE: Gold there is, and rubies in abundance, but lips that speak knowledge are a rare jewel. (Prov. 20:15)

Ammiel (M/F)

MEANING: "people of God"

SIGNIFICANCE: In the Bible, Ammiel was the sixth son of Obed-edom. His family served as gatekeepers in the temple during the reign of King David.

KEY VERSE: I will walk among you; I will be your God, and you will be my people. (Lev. 26:12 NLT)

Amoret (SEE AIMEE)

Amos (M)

MEANING: "burden carrier"

SIGNIFICANCE: Amos was a prophet to Israel who called for justice and an end to the mistreatment of the poor. He is the author of the biblical book that bears his name.

KEY VERSE: Praise be to the Lord, to God our Savior, who daily bears our burdens. (Ps. 68:19)

Anastasia (F)

MEANING: "resurrection"

SIGNIFICANCE: Saint Anastasia (died c. 304) was a spiritual student of Saint Chrysogonus and martyred in the persecutions of Roman emperor Diocletian.

KEY VERSE: Praise be to the God and Father of our Lord Jesus Christ! In his great mercy he has given us new birth into a living hope through the resurrection of Jesus Christ. (1 Peter 1:3)

Anatolia (F)

MEANING: "rising of the sun"

SIGNIFICANCE: When Saint Anatolia (died 250) refused to marry a persistent suitor, she was denounced for her faith. She was arrested and placed in a room with a venomous snake. When her executioner saw that she was unharmed, he became a Christian and was martyred as well.

KEY VERSE: From the rising of the sun to the place where it sets, the name of the LORD is to be praised. (Ps. 113:3)

Anders (SEE ANDREW)

Andre (SEE ANDREW)

Andreas (SEE ANDREW)

Andres (SEE ANDREW)

A

Andrew (M)

MEANING: "strong"; "manly"

SIGNIFICANCE: In the Bible, Andrew was one of the twelve apostles. He is noted for bringing people to Jesus—his brother Peter, the boy with the fish and bread at the feeding of the five thousand, and the Greeks who approached Philip with a request to see Jesus.

KEY VERSE: It is God who arms me with strength and makes my way perfect. (Ps. 18:32)

Andrique (SEE HENRY)

Andrius (SEE ANDREW)

Angel (F)

MEANING: "messenger"

SIGNIFICANCE: According to the Bible, angels have many tasks, including worshipping, guiding, protecting, and encouraging, but their overarching purpose is to serve God.

KEY VERSE: I have not kept the good news of your justice hidden in my heart; I have talked about your faithfulness and saving power. I have told everyone in the great assembly of your unfailing love and faithfulness. (Ps. 40:10 NLT)

Angela (F)

MEANING: "angel"; "messenger"

SIGNIFICANCE: As a young woman, Saint Angela Merici (1474–1540) received a vision telling her she would inspire devout women in their vocation. Several years later, she founded the first order of women teachers, the Ursuline Sisters.

KEY VERSE: Like the coolness of snow at harvest time is a trustworthy messenger to those who send him. (Prov. 25:13)

Angelana (SEE ANGELA)

Angelo (M)

MEANING: "messenger of God"

SIGNIFICANCE: Saint Angelo Carletti di Chivasso (1411–95) was a noted theologian and served as a papal nuncio (diplomatic representative) for Pope Sixtus IV and Pope Innocent VIII. He wrote *Cases of Conscience*, a dictionary of moral theology.

KEY VERSE: Give thanks to the LORD, call on his name; make known among the nations what he has done. (Ps. 105:1)

Aniol (SEE ANGELO)

Anna (F)

MEANING: "graceful"

SIGNIFICANCE: In the Bible, Anna is remembered for living a life of worship and devotion to God, and for testifying of Jesus' birth to "all who were looking forward to the redemption of Jerusalem."

KEY VERSE: A woman of gentle grace gets respect. (Prov. 11:16 MSG)

Annetta (F)

MEANING: "God has favored me"

SIGNIFICANCE: Saint Annetta Bentivoglio (1834–1905) became a Poor Clare nun at age thirty. She found the discipline difficult, but saw it as a way to reach God, and practiced strict observance to the Rule. In 1875 she was sent to America to institute the Poor Clares there. Some clerics told her group they would fail, that the contemplative life was not suited

to Americans, but the sisters pressed on, founding houses in Nebraska,
Louisiana, and Indiana—always in the face of opposition, with little
support, and with Annetta's health failing.

KEY VERSE: The LORD God is a sun and shield; the LORD bestows favor
and honor; no good thing does he withhold from those whose walk is
blameless. (Ps. 84:11)

Anselm (M)

MEANING: "divine warrior"

SIGNIFICANCE: Anselm of Canterbury (1033–1109) is known as the
founder of Scholasticism, which, in part, attempts to use logic to
understand faith. He believed the existence of the idea of God
necessarily implied the actual existence of God.

KEY VERSE: Praise be to the LORD my Rock, who trains my hands for war,
my fingers for battle. (Ps. 144:1)

Antek (SEE ANTHONY)

Anthony (M)

MEANING: "priceless"

SIGNIFICANCE: Saint Anthony of Padua (1195–1231) is one of the
most famous of Roman Catholic saints. He is said to have been an
eloquent speaker and teacher of theology and attracted crowds
everywhere he went. Legend has it that even the fish loved to listen to
him preach.

KEY VERSE: Wisdom is supreme; therefore get wisdom. Though it cost all
you have, get understanding. (Prov. 4:7)

Antoine (SEE ANTHONY)

A

Anton (M)

MEANING: "worthy of praise"

SIGNIFICANCE: Anton Chekhov (1860–1905) was a Russian playwright and short-story writer who profoundly influenced both genres. One of his best-known contributions is Chekhov's Gun: "If you say in the first chapter that there is a rifle hanging on the wall, in the second or third chapter it absolutely must go off. If it's not going to be fired, it shouldn't be hanging there."

KEY VERSE: Great is the LORD and most worthy of praise; his greatness no one can fathom. (Ps. 145:3)

Antonina (F)

MEANING: "praiseworthy"

SIGNIFICANCE: Saint Antonina (died 306) was martyred for refusing to sacrifice to pagan gods.

KEY VERSE: Praise the LORD, all his works everywhere in his dominion. Praise the LORD, O my soul. (Ps. 103:22)

Anysia (F)

MEANING: "complete"

SIGNIFICANCE: Born to a wealthy and pious family, Anysia (died 304) lived private vows of chastity and poverty, praying and using her wealth to help the poor.

KEY VERSE: May God, who gives this patience and encouragement, help you live in complete harmony with each other, as is fitting for followers of Christ Jesus. (Rom. 15:5 NLT)

Anzhel (SEE ANGELO)

A

Aphra (SEE AFRA)

Aquila (M)

MEANING: "eagle"

SIGNIFICANCE: In the Bible, Aquila, and his wife, Priscilla, were loyal friends and trusted coworkers of the apostle Paul.

KEY VERSE: Those who hope in the LORD will renew their strength. They will soar on wings like eagles; they will run and not grow weary, they will walk and not be faint. (Isa. 40:31)

Ara (M/F)

MEANING: "altar"

SIGNIFICANCE: In the Bible, Ara was a chief in the tribe of Asher.

KEY VERSE: I will sacrifice a freewill offering to you; I will praise your name, O LORD, for it is good. (Ps. 54:6)

Aram (M)

MEANING: "high place"

SIGNIFICANCE: In the Bible, Aram was a grandson of Noah.

KEY VERSE: Mightier than the thunder of the great waters, mightier than the breakers of the sea—the LORD on high is mighty. (Ps. 93:4)

Aran (M)

MEANING: "nimble"

SIGNIFICANCE: In the Bible, Aran was a descendant of Esau.

KEY VERSE: Everyone should be quick to listen, slow to speak and slow to become angry. (James 1:19)

Archer (M)

MEANING: "bowman"

SIGNIFICANCE: Many legends and stories have archers as main characters. Upon his return, Odysseus reestablished himself in his home using his ability with his bow. Tradition holds that an archer named Hercules founded the ancient Olympic games. Robin Hood and William Tell gained fame through target archery.

KEY VERSE: Who is God besides the LORD? ... He trains my hands for battle; my arms can bend a bow of bronze. (Ps. 18:31, 34)

Ardon (M)

MEANING: "subduer"; "bronze"

SIGNIFICANCE: Ardon was the son of Caleb, who was sent by Moses to evaluate the Promised Land.

KEY VERSE: He is my loving God and my fortress, my stronghold and my deliverer, my shield, in whom I take refuge, who subdues peoples under me. (Ps. 144:2)

Aria (F)

MEANING: "air"

SIGNIFICANCE: An aria is a complex melody composed for one voice, usually accompanied by an orchestra.

KEY VERSE: By day the LORD directs his love, at night his song is with me—a prayer to the God of my life. (Ps. 42:8)

Arianell (F)

MEANING: "silver"

SIGNIFICANCE: Arianell was a sixth-century nun and spiritual student of Saint Dyfrig.

KEY VERSE: A good name is more desirable than great riches; to be esteemed is better than silver or gold. (Prov. 22:1)

Ariel (F)

MEANING: "lion [lioness] of God"

SIGNIFICANCE: In the Bible, Ariel was a messenger sent by Ezra.

KEY VERSE: The righteous are as bold as a lion. (Prov. 28:1)

Aristeo (SEE ARISTO)

Aristo (M/F)

MEANING: "best"

SIGNIFICANCE: Originally, this name was a prefix intended to show that the person named was the best. Aristophanes was a Greek writer of comedy. Aristotle was one of the great ancient Greek philosophers.

KEY VERSE: Do your best to present yourself to God as one approved. (2 Tim. 2:15)

Armand (M)

MEANING: "soldier"

SIGNIFICANCE: Saint Armand of Maire was a sixth-century abbot of a monastery and supported monastic expansion and evangelization in his region.

KEY VERSE: With your help I can advance against a troop; with my God I can scale a wall. (Ps. 18:29)

Armando (SEE ARMAND)

Aron (SEE AARON)

Arrian (SEE ADRIAN)

A

Arsenius (M)

MEANING: "masculine"

SIGNIFICANCE: Saint Arsenius (died c. 450) was a deacon and tutor to the sons of Emperor Theodosius the Great. He said, "I have often been sorry for having spoken, but never for having held my tongue."

KEY VERSE: The mouth of the righteous man utters wisdom, and his tongue speaks what is just. (Ps. 37:30)

Artek (SEE ARTHUR)

Arthur (M)

MEANING: "bear"; "stone"

SIGNIFICANCE: The legendary King Arthur personifies wisdom and fairness. His stories represent him as the ideal king in both war and peace.

KEY VERSE: The LORD has become my fortress, and my God the rock in whom I take refuge. (Ps. 94:22)

Arwen (F)

MEANING: "royal maiden"

SIGNIFICANCE: Arwen is a fictional character appearing in J. R. R. Tolkien's fantasy series The Lord of the Rings. She is a half-elf and gives up her elvish immortality to marry Aragorn, King of the Reunited Kingdom.

KEY VERSE: GOD made the heavens—royal splendor radiates from him, a powerful beauty sets him apart. (Ps. 96:5–6 MSG)

Asa (M/F)

MEANING: "physician"

SIGNIFICANCE: In the Bible, Asa was a godly king of Judah who cleared the land of pagan shrines and statues.

KEY VERSE: Heal me, O LORD, and I will be healed; save me and I will be saved, for you are the one I praise. (Jer. 17:14)

Asaiah (M)

MEANING: "the Lord has made"

SIGNIFICANCE: In the Bible, Asaiah was a priestly leader in the time of King David and helped bring the ark of the covenant to Jerusalem.

KEY VERSE: The LORD has made everything for his own purposes. (Prov. 16:4 NLT)

Asarelah (M)

MEANING: "right toward God"

SIGNIFICANCE: In the Bible, Asarelah was one of Asaph's four sons appointed by David to help with prophecy and music in the sanctuary.

KEY VERSE: You may fall on your knees and pray—to God's delight! You'll see God's smile and celebrate, finding yourself set right with God. (Job 33:26 MSG)

Asher (M/F)

MEANING: "happy"

SIGNIFICANCE: In the Bible, Asher was a son of Jacob, born to Leah's maid, Zilpah. The boy was given his name because his mother was so happy at his birth.

KEY VERSE: Worship the LORD with gladness; come before him with joyful songs. (Ps. 100:2)

Astevan (SEE STEPHEN)

A

Atarah (F)

MEANING: "crown"

SIGNIFICANCE: In the Bible, Atarah was the wife of a descendant of Caleb, one of the two spies Moses sent into the Promised Land who came back with confidence that God would give the land to the Israelites.

KEY VERSE: Blessings crown the head of the righteous. (Prov. 10:6)

Athan (M)

MEANING: "immortal"

SIGNIFICANCE: Saint Athan (fifth century–sixth century) founded both a monastery and a school and was noted for his gentleness and generosity.

KEY VERSE: He crowns you with love and mercy—a paradise crown. He wraps you in goodness—beauty eternal. (Ps. 103:4–5 MSG)

Athanasia (F)

MEANING: "immortal"

SIGNIFICANCE: Athanasia was a first-century saint and martyr.

KEY VERSE: I will make you an eternal excellence, a joy of many generations. (Isa. 60:15 NKJV)

Aubert (M)

MEANING: "noble and bright"

SIGNIFICANCE: Bishop Aubert (died c. 669) founded several monasteries in Flanders and Hainault.

KEY VERSE: You'll do best by filling your minds and meditating on things true, noble, reputable, authentic, compelling, gracious—the best, not the worst; the beautiful, not the ugly; things to praise, not things to curse. (Phil. 4:8 MSG)

Audra (SEE AUDREY)

Audrey (F)

MEANING: "noble strength"

SIGNIFICANCE: Saint Audrey (c. 640–79) enjoyed showing off her wealth by wearing extravagant jewelry. After her conversion, however, she lived an austere life, willingly accepting penance for her pride.

KEY VERSE: God is my strength and power, and He makes my way perfect. (2 Sam. 22:33 NKJV)

Augustin (SEE AUGUSTUS, AUGUSTINE)

Augustine (M)

MEANING: "magnificent"

SIGNIFICANCE: Saint Augustine (354–430) is considered by many to be the greatest and most influential theologian of the Western church and is most famous for his writings on salvation and grace.

KEY VERSE: GOD is magnificent; he can never be praised enough. There are no boundaries to his greatness. (Ps. 145:3 MSG)

Augustus (M)

MEANING: "great"

SIGNIFICANCE: Saint Augustus (died fifth century) was driven from his homeland for his faith and spent the rest of his life in another region as a preacher and evangelist.

KEY VERSE: Great is the LORD! He is most worthy of praise! No one can measure his greatness. (Ps. 145:3 NLT)

A

Aurea (F)

MEANING: "gold"

SIGNIFICANCE: Aurea of San Millán (c. 1042–69) was a Benedictine nun and hermit, also a spiritual student of Saint Dominic of Silos.

KEY VERSE: The Almighty will be your gold and your precious silver. (Job 22:25 NKJV)

Aurelius (M)

MEANING: "gold"

SIGNIFICANCE: Saint Aurelius (died 852) was raised as a secret Christian and didn't proclaim his faith until, as an adult, he saw a local merchant beaten to death for being a Christian. Eventually, Aurelius and his wife, Natalia, were martyred for their faith.

KEY VERSE: You'll be a stunning crown in the palm of GOD's hand, a jeweled gold cup held high in the hand of your God. (Isa. 62:3 MSG)

Austin (SEE AUGUSTUS)

Avery (SEE ALFRED)

Avva (F)

MEANING: "mother"

SIGNIFICANCE: In the Bible, Avva is a city.

KEY VERSE: I have calmed and quieted myself, like a weaned child who no longer cries for its mother's milk. (Ps. 131:2 NLT)

Azusa (M/F)

MEANING: "place of water"

SIGNIFICANCE: The famous Azusa Street Revival, which continued for

A

three and a half years, brought unprecedented recognition to Pentecostalism.

KEY VERSE: The LORD is my shepherd, I shall not be in want. He makes me lie down in green pastures, he leads me beside quiet waters. (Ps. 23:1–2)

B

"REMEMBER THAT A MAN'S
NAME IS, TO HIM, THE
SWEETEST AND MOST
IMPORTANT SOUND IN ANY
LANGUAGE."

— DALE CARNEGIE

Babbie (SEE BARBARA)

Babs (SEE BARBARA)

Bailintin (SEE VALENTINE)

Balin (M)

MEANING: "mighty warrior"

SIGNIFICANCE: Saint Balin (seventh century) was one of four sons of an Anglo-Saxon king who accompanied Saint Colman to Iona and then retired to Connaught.

KEY VERSE: Give unto the LORD, O you mighty ones, give unto the LORD glory and strength. (Ps. 29:1 NKJV)

Baltasar (M)

MEANING: "protected by God"

SIGNIFICANCE: Baltasar Gracian (1601–58), a Spanish Jesuit writer, is best known for his work *The Art of Worldly Wisdom,* a compilation of advice for success in the world.

KEY VERSE: I will lie down and sleep, for you alone, O LORD, will keep me safe. (Ps. 4:8 NLT)

Bani (M/F)

MEANING: "build"

SIGNIFICANCE: In the Bible, Bani was one of David's thirty-seven warriors.

KEY VERSE: Unless the LORD builds a house, the work of the builders is wasted. (Ps. 127:1 NLT)

Banner (M)

MEANING: "flag"; "standard"

SIGNIFICANCE: Throughout history, banners have been used for identification during battles and as rallying points for soldiers.

KEY VERSE: We will shout for joy when you [God] are victorious and will lift up our banners in the name of our God. May the LORD grant all your requests. (Ps. 20:5)

Barak (M)

MEANING: "flash of lightning"

SIGNIFICANCE: Barak was an associate of the prophetess Deborah and led an Israelite army to defeat the Canaanites. He is listed in Hebrews 11 as a hero of the faith.

KEY VERSE: Have mercy on me, O God, have mercy! ... I will hide beneath the shadow of your wings until the danger passes by. (Ps. 57:1 NLT)

Barbara (F)

MEANING: "mysterious"

SIGNIFICANCE: The legendary Saint Barbara converted to Christianity with the help of Origen and was martyred for her faith. As she died, her killer was immediately struck by lightning.

KEY VERSE: The LORD is a friend to those who fear him. He teaches them his covenant. (Ps. 25:14 NLT)

Barnabas (M)

MEANING: "son of prophecy"

SIGNIFICANCE: In the Bible, Barnabas was the first to travel with Paul as a missionary team. In Acts he is mentioned as "a good man, full of the Holy Spirit and of faith" (11:24 RSV).

KEY VERSE: Preach the Word; be prepared in season and out of season; correct, rebuke and encourage—with great patience and careful instruction. (2 Tim. 4:2)

Barnaby (SEE BARNABAS)

Barrick (SEE BARAK)

Barry (SEE BENEDICT)

Bart (SEE BARTHOLOMEW)

Bartholomew (M)

MEANING: "son of a farmer"

SIGNIFICANCE: Saint Bartholomew Longo

(1841–1926) was raised in a godly home but turned from the faith as a young adult. Friends and family prayed tirelessly for him, and he eventually embraced Christianity once again. Wanting to make amends for his wasted years, Bartholomew established a trade school for boys whose fathers were in jail, successfully disproving the then-popular assumption that children of criminals were themselves doomed to be criminals.

KEY VERSE: He who sows righteousness gets a true reward. (Prov. 11:18 NASB)

Baruch (M)

MEANING: "blessed"

SIGNIFICANCE: In the Bible, Baruch was the faithful secretary of the prophet Jeremiah who recorded unpopular—yet truthful—prophecies.

KEY VERSE: You're blessed when you stay on course, walking steadily on the road revealed by GOD. (Ps. 119:1 MSG)

Basil (M)

MEANING: "royal"

SIGNIFICANCE: Saint Basil the Great (329–79) left his law practice to become a monk. He founded and directed a monastery and wrote a famous monastic rule that lasted longer than any other in the East.

KEY VERSE: He who keeps a royal command experiences no trouble, for a wise heart knows the proper time and procedure. (Eccl. 8:5 NASB)

Basilio (SEE BASIL)

Basto (SEE SEBASTIAN)

Bat (SEE BARTHOLOMEW)

Baxter (M)

MEANING: "baker"

SIGNIFICANCE: Puritan author Richard Baxter (1615–91) is best known for his influential work, *The Saints' Everlasting Rest,* which discusses the nature of life after death.

KEY VERSE: Generous hands are blessed hands because they give bread to the poor. (Prov. 22:9 MSG)

Bea (SEE BEATRICE, BEATRIX)

Beatrex (SEE BEATRIX)

Beatrice (F)

MEANING: "voyager"

SIGNIFICANCE: Saint Beatrice (1424–90) was raised in the household of Princess Isabel but tired of the royal life. She dedicated the rest of her life to God and eventually founded a new order of nuns.

KEY VERSE: From now on every road you travel will take you to GOD. Follow the Covenant signs; read the charted directions. (Ps. 25:10 MSG)

Beatrissa (SEE BEATRICE)

Beatrix (F)

MEANING: "blessed"

SIGNIFICANCE: Beatrix Potter (1866–1943) was a British writer and illustrator of children's books best known for her story *The Tale of Peter Rabbit*.

KEY VERSE: You're blessed when you stay on course, walking steadily on the road revealed by GOD. (Ps. 119:1 MSG)

Becca (SEE REBECCA)

Becket (M)

MEANING: "brook"

SIGNIFICANCE: Thomas Becket (1118–70) became archbishop of Canterbury in 1162. Becket championed the rights of the people and fought to preserve the position of the church in society.

KEY VERSE: As the deer pants for the water brooks, so pants my soul for You, O God. (Ps. 42:1 NKJV)

Beckie, Becky (SEE REBECCA)

B

Bela (M/F)

MEANING: "intelligent"

SIGNIFICANCE: In the Bible, Bela was the oldest son of Benjamin, Jacob's youngest and favorite son.

KEY VERSE: Intelligent people are always ready to learn. Their ears are open for knowledge. (Prov. 18:15 NLT)

Belicia (SEE ISABEL)

Belina (F)

MEANING: "beautiful"

SIGNIFICANCE: Saint Belina (died 1135) was a peasant girl who was martyred for her beliefs.

KEY VERSE: Let the beauty of the LORD our God be upon us, and establish the work of our hands for us. (Ps. 90:17 NKJV)

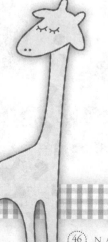

Benjamin (M)

MEANING: "son of my right hand"

SIGNIFICANCE: In the Bible, Benjamin was the youngest son of Jacob and a skilled warrior.

KEY VERSE: I have set the LORD always before me. Because he is at my right hand, I will not be shaken. (Ps. 16:8)

B

Beno (M)

MEANING: "his son"

SIGNIFICANCE: In the Bible, Beno was a Levite assigned to temple duty.

KEY VERSE: Those who are led by the Spirit of God are sons of God. (Rom. 8:14)

Berea (M/F)

MEANING: "weighty"; "heavy"

SIGNIFICANCE: In the Bible, those living in the city of Berea were said to be of "noble character" because they searched the Scriptures to see if the apostle Paul was teaching the truth (Acts 17:11).

KEY VERSE: Jesus said, "Come to me, all of you who are weary and carry heavy burdens, and I will give you rest." (Matt. 11:28 NLT)

Beret (SEE BRIDGET)

Bergette (SEE BRIDGET)

Beri (M)

MEANING: "my son"

SIGNIFICANCE: In the Bible, Beri was a descendent of Asher, son of Jacob, and is noted as a skilled warrior.

KEY VERSE: Those who are led by the Spirit of God are sons of God. (Rom. 8:14)

B

Bernadette (F)

MEANING: "bold as a bear"

SIGNIFICANCE: Saint Bernadette of Lourdes (1844–79) is credited with several visions of the Virgin Mary. She taught the merits of prayer, penance, poverty, and church.

KEY VERSE: In the day when I cried out, You answered me, and made me bold with strength in my soul. (Ps. 138:3 NKJV)

Bernard (M)

MEANING: "bold as a bear"

SIGNIFICANCE: Saint Bernard of Clairvaux (1090–1153) began each day with a question: "Why have I come here?" His answer: "to lead a holy life." He purposed to use his talents, resources, and experiences for God so that no day would be wasted.

KEY VERSE: In the day when I cried out, You answered me, and made me bold with strength in my soul. (Ps. 138:3 NKJV)

Bernetta (SEE BERNADETTE)

Bernice (F)

MEANING: "bringer of victory"

SIGNIFICANCE: In the Bible, Bernice was the oldest daughter of Herod Agrippa I and was present during the apostle Paul's speech before her brother

King Agrippa II. In AD 66, Bernice bravely yet unsuccessfully appealed to the Roman curator Gessius Florus not to ransack the temple in Jerusalem.

KEY VERSE: Everyone runs; one wins. Run to win. (1 Cor. 9:24 MSG)

Bernita (SEE BERNADETTE)

Bess (SEE ELIZABETH)

Besse, Bessie, Bessy (SEE ELIZABETH)

Betha (SEE ELIZABETH)

Bethany (F)

MEANING: "house of song"

SIGNIFICANCE: In the Bible, Bethany was the home of Jesus' friends Mary, Martha, and Lazarus.

KEY VERSE: Each day the LORD pours his unfailing love upon me, and through each night I sing his songs, praying to God who gives me life. (Ps. 42:8 NLT)

Bethel (M/F)

MEANING: "house of God"

SIGNIFICANCE: In the Bible, Bethel was the place where Jacob dreamed of a stairway to heaven on which angels were ascending and descending. In the dream, God promised his presence and blessing to Jacob.

KEY VERSE: Your beauty and love chase after me every day of my life. I'm back home in the house of GOD for the rest of my life. (Ps. 23:6 MSG)

Betsy (F)

MEANING: "oath of God"

SIGNIFICANCE: According to legend, Betsy Ross (1752–1836) designed and sewed the first American flag, which was flown on July 8, 1776, when the Declaration of Independence was read aloud at Independence Hall.

KEY VERSE: I have taken an oath and confirmed it, that I will follow your righteous laws. (Ps. 119:106)

Beulah (F)

MEANING: "married"

SIGNIFICANCE: In the Bible, the land of Israel is called Beulah. In John Bunyan's *Pilgrim's Progress*, Beulah is the land of peace.

KEY VERSE: He who finds a wife finds what is good and receives favor from the LORD. (Prov. 18:22)

Bibiana (SEE VIVIANA)

Bice (SEE BEATRICE)

Billy (M)

MEANING: "resolute protector"

SIGNIFICANCE: Billy Sunday (1863–1935) was first noted as a professional baseball player for the Chicago White Stockings. At a service at the Pacific Garden Mission, he became a Christian, and soon quit baseball to become a street minister for the YMCA in Chicago. He grew to be the most successful evangelist prior to World War I.

KEY VERSE: Let all who take refuge in you rejoice; let them sing joyful praises forever. Spread your protection over them, that all who love your name may be filled with joy. (Ps. 5:11 NLT)

Birget, Birgetta (SEE BRIDGET)

Blaise (M)

MEANING: "cleric"

SIGNIFICANCE: Blaise Pascal (1623–62) was a French mathematician, physicist, and Christian philosopher. "Pascal's Wager" is a challenge to believe in God. "If you gain, you gain all; if you lose, you lose nothing. Wager, then, without hesitation that He is."

KEY VERSE: Protect me, for I am devoted to you. Save me, for I serve you and trust you. You are my God. (Ps. 86:2 NLT)

Blake (M)

MEANING: "shining white"

SIGNIFICANCE: English poet William Blake (1757–1827) wrote, printed, and hand-colored his own books, now considered priceless works of art. His statement, "If the doors of perception were cleansed, every thing would appear to man as it is, infinite" is foundational to the modern definition of imagination.

KEY VERSE: Let your face shine on your servant; save me in your unfailing love. (Ps. 31:16)

Blanchard (M)

MEANING: "white"

SIGNIFICANCE: Jonathan Blanchard (1811–92) was a pastor, educator, social reformer, abolitionist, and the first president of Wheaton College.

KEY VERSE: All who are victorious will be clothed in white. I will never erase their names from the Book of Life, but I will announce before my Father and his angels that they are mine. (Rev. 3:5 NLT)

Blane (M)

MEANING: "strong one"

SIGNIFICANCE: Saint Blane (died c. 590) was a Scottish monk, missionary, and later bishop.

B

Tradition says he traveled safely from Ireland to Scotland in a boat without oars or rudder.

KEY VERSE: Wait on the LORD; be of good courage, and He shall strengthen your heart; wait, I say, on the LORD! (Ps. 27:14 NKJV)

Bloom (F)

MEANING: "flower"

SIGNIFICANCE: This name honors the phrase "Bloom where you're planted," meaning, make a difference wherever you find yourself.

KEY VERSE: As the earth bursts with spring wildflowers, and as a garden cascades with blossoms, so the Master, GOD, brings righteousness into full bloom and puts praise on display before the nations. (Isa. 61:11 MSG)

Blossom (F)

MEANING: "flowering"

SIGNIFICANCE: A blossom is a delicate flower that precedes fruit on a tree.

KEY VERSE: I am the vine; you are the branches. If a man remains in me and I in him, he will bear much fruit; apart from me you can do nothing. (John 15:5)

Booth (M)

MEANING: "herald"

SIGNIFICANCE: William (1829–1912) and Catherine Booth founded the Salvation Army in 1865 as a means to meet the physical and spiritual needs of the poor and disenfranchised. As both a Protestant denomination and a social-relief agency, it currently operates in more than 111 countries and 175 languages and is, after the United Nations, the world's largest provider of social aid.

KEY VERSE: How lovely on the mountains are the feet of him who brings good news, who announces peace and brings good news of happiness, who announces salvation. (Isa. 52:7 NASB)

Boyd (M)
MEANING: "blond"

SIGNIFICANCE: Zachary Boyd (1585–1653) was a Scottish religious writer whose ambition was to put the entire Bible into verse. While he was unable to accomplish this goal, his biblical poetry, especially his rendition of the Twenty-third Psalm, is still revered today.

KEY VERSE: You will be like the wings of a dove covered with silver, and her feathers with yellow gold. (Ps. 68:13 NKJV)

Bram (SEE ABRAHAM)

Brandan (M)
MEANING: "sword"

SIGNIFICANCE: Saint Brandan (fifth century) was an Irish monk who migrated to Britain. He was persecuted there and sought refuge in a monastery in Gaul, where he stayed and eventually became abbot.

KEY VERSE: Put on salvation as your helmet, and take the sword of the Spirit, which is the word of God. (Eph. 6:17 NLT)

Branham (M)

MEANING: "raven estate"

SIGNIFICANCE: William Branham (1909–65) was a Pentecostal preacher who emphasized healing. His ministry filled stadiums and auditoriums all over the world.

KEY VERSE: Consider the ravens: They do not sow or reap, they have no storeroom or barn; yet God feeds them. And how much more valuable you are than birds! (Luke 12:24)

Braulio (M)

MEANING: "glowing"

SIGNIFICANCE: Saint Braulio (c. 590–c. 651) was archbishop of Zaragoza and a noted scholar, writer, and correspondent.

KEY VERSE: The ways of right-living people glow with light; the longer they live, the brighter they shine. (Prov. 4:18 MSG)

Brenach (M)

MEANING: "damp"

SIGNIFICANCE: Saint Brenach was a contemporary of Saint Patrick. His missionary efforts in Wales resulted in many conversions, including Brecan, ruler of South Wales, who then founded many churches there.

KEY VERSE: The generous man will be prosperous, and he who waters will himself be watered. (Prov. 11:25 NASB)

Brendan (M)

MEANING: "sword"

SIGNIFICANCE: Saint Brendan (460–c. 577) and a group of other Irish monks are said to have sailed across the Atlantic in a ship made of ox hides nearly a thousand years before Columbus made his historic voyage of discovery.

KEY VERSE: Put on salvation as your helmet, and take the sword of the Spirit, which is the word of God. (Eph. 6:17 NLT)

Brian (M)

MEANING: "honorable"

SIGNIFICANCE: Saint Brian Lacey (died 1591) was arrested and condemned to death for his faith and for aiding priests.

KEY VERSE: My victory and honor come from God

alone. He is my refuge, a rock where no enemy can reach me. (Ps. 62:7 NLT)

Briant (M)

MEANING: "strong"

SIGNIFICANCE: Saint Alexander Briant (1556–81) was an English Jesuit who, when martyred, felt no pain during the tortures. He said: "Whether this that I say be miraculous or no, God knows."

KEY VERSE: Wait on the LORD; be of good courage, and He shall strengthen your heart; wait, I say, on the LORD! (Ps. 27:14 NKJV)

Brice (M/F)

MEANING: "son of a nobleman"

SIGNIFICANCE: Saint Brice (died 444) was an orphan raised by Saint Martin of Tours. His wild behavior and ungrateful attitude prompted many to advise Martin to send him away. Martin responded, "If Jesus could deal with Judas, I can deal with Brice." Over the next several years, Brice changed his ways and began to lead a pious and admirable life. It took many years, however, for his public reputation to change.

KEY VERSE: The noble man makes noble plans, and by noble deeds he stands. (Isa. 32:8)

Bridget (F)

MEANING: "high one"

SIGNIFICANCE: Saint Bridget of Sweden (c. 1303–73) was a friend and counselor to many priests and theologians. Her writings of her visions were hugely popular in the Middle Ages. Bridget encouraged all who would listen to meditate on the Passion of Christ.

KEY VERSE: My shield is God Most High, who saves the upright in heart. (Ps. 7:10)

Brigid (F)

MEANING: "fiery arrow"

SIGNIFICANCE: Saint Brigid of Ireland (453–523) was born to an Irish king, whom, tradition says, she regularly annoyed by giving away food and possessions to the poor. She became a nun and eventually founded both a school of art and a double monastery of nuns and monks.

KEY VERSE: My question: What are God-worshipers like? Your answer: Arrows aimed at God's bull's-eye. (Ps. 25:12 MSG)

Brogan (M/F)

MEANING: "terror"

SIGNIFICANCE: Brogan was a sixth- or seventh-century

scribe and bishop of Mothil, Waterford, Ireland, and may have been the nephew of Saint Patrick.

KEY VERSE: Do not be afraid of sudden terror, nor of trouble from the wicked when it comes. (Prov. 3:25 NKJV)

Bronson (SEE BRUNO)

Brook (F)

MEANING: "stream"

SIGNIFICANCE: In the Bible, the prophet Elijah was miraculously fed by ravens during a time of drought as he rested by a brook.

KEY VERSE: As the deer pants for the water brooks, so pants my soul for You, O God. (Ps. 42:1 NKJV)

Bruce (M)

MEANING: "thick brush"

SIGNIFICANCE: Robert the Bruce, King of Scotland (fourteenth century), learned the value of perseverance from watching a spider spin a web.

KEY VERSE: So you'll go out in joy, you'll be led into a whole and complete life. The mountains and hills will lead the parade, bursting with song. All the trees of the forest will join the procession, exuberant with applause. (Isa. 55:12 MSG)

B

Bruin (SEE BRUNO)

Bruno (M)

MEANING: "brown" (usually associated with brown bears)

SIGNIFICANCE: Saint Bruno (1030–1101) was a teacher of theology, and one of his students later became Pope Urban II. He founded a monastery in which he and his fellow monks supported themselves as manuscript copyists.

KEY VERSE: [God] made all the stars—the Bear and Orion, the Pleiades and the constellations of the southern sky. He does great things too marvelous to understand. (Job 9:9–10 NLT)

Bryant (SEE BRIANT)

C

"REMEMBER THAT A MAN'S NAME IS, TO HIM, THE SWEETEST AND MOST IMPORTANT SOUND IN ANY LANGUAGE."

— DALE CARNEGIE

C

Cabot (M)

MEANING: "to sail"

SIGNIFICANCE: Explorer John Cabot (c. 1450–c. 1499) is commonly credited as the first modern European to have discovered the North American mainland.

KEY VERSE: You faithfully answer our prayers with awesome deeds, O God our Savior. You are the hope of everyone on earth, even those who sail on distant seas. (Ps. 65:5 NLT)

Cacilia (SEE CECILIA)

Cadoc (M)

MEANING: "battle"

SIGNIFICANCE: Saint Cadoc of Llancarvan (died c. 580) was raised by an Irish monk and became a priest. Legend has it that he saved his brother monks from starvation by tying a white thread to the foot of a well-fed mouse. He then followed the thread to an abandoned, well-stocked granary.

KEY VERSE: O Sovereign LORD, the strong one who rescued me, you protected me on the day of battle. (Ps. 140:7 NLT)

Caedmon (M)

MEANING: "poet"

SIGNIFICANCE: Saint Caedmon (died c. 670)

received a vision in which he was commanded to glorify God with hymns. As he was illiterate, his monk brothers would read the Bible to him, and Caedmon would say it back to them in poetry.

KEY VERSE: Beautiful words stir my heart. I will recite a lovely poem about the king, for my tongue is like the pen of a skillful poet. (Ps. 45:1 NLT)

Caillin (M/F)

MEANING: "child"

SIGNIFICANCE: Saint Caillin (seventh century) was a bishop who, according to legend, turned some aggressive Druids into stone.

KEY VERSE: Even a child is known by his actions, by whether his conduct is pure and right. (Prov. 20:11)

Caimin (M/F)

MEANING: "sanctuary"

SIGNIFICANCE: Saint Caimin (died c. 650) was well educated and maintained a reputation of holiness that attracted students to him.

KEY VERSE: Your way, O God, is in the sanctuary; who is so great a God as our God? (Ps. 77:13 NKJV)

Cairistiona (SEE CHRISTINA)

Caitlin (SEE CATHERINE)

Caitria (SEE CATHERINE)

C

Caleb (M)

MEANING: "bold"

SIGNIFICANCE: In the Bible, Caleb was one of the scouts sent by Moses to survey the Promised Land. Because of his faith in God's promises, he was one of only two adults allowed to enter the land.

KEY VERSE: When I called, you answered me; you made me bold and stouthearted. (Ps. 138:3)

Callisto (M)

MEANING: "most beautiful"

SIGNIFICANCE: Saint Callisto (1903–30) was a fervent and faithful missionary to China who was brutally murdered as he tried to protect a young student from bandits.

KEY VERSE: Praise the LORD! For it is good to sing praises to our God; for it is pleasant, and praise is beautiful. (Ps. 147:1 NKJV)

Calvin (M)

MEANING: "bald"

SIGNIFICANCE: John Calvin (1509–64) was a brilliant theologian with a heart for the church and a broad knowledge of the Bible. His volumes of theology—*Institutes of the Christian Religion*—are regarded as a classic to this day.

KEY VERSE: Your word I have treasured in my heart, that I may not sin against You. (Ps. 119:11 NASB)

Camilla (F)

MEANING: "noble"

SIGNIFICANCE: Saint Camilla (died 437) was a disciple of Saint Germain of Auxerre.

KEY VERSE: Whatever is true, whatever is noble, whatever is right, whatever is pure, whatever is lovely, whatever is admirable—if anything is excellent or praiseworthy—think about such things. (Phil. 4:8)

Camille (SEE CAMILLA)

Candace (F)

MEANING: "glittering"; "flowing white"

SIGNIFICANCE: Candace (or Kandake) was a title given to Ethiopian queens, much the same as Pharaoh was to Egyptian kings. The queen mentioned in Acts 8 came to Jerusalem with a particular eunuch. This man met with the apostle Philip and understood God's Word for the first time. Perhaps this encounter helped to spread the good news to yet another part of the world.

KEY VERSE: Where the river flows everything will live. (Ezek. 47:9)

C

Canice (M/F)

MEANING: "good-looking"

SIGNIFICANCE: Saint Canice (c. 525–c. 599) was known as an effective preacher and missionary. According to legend, when he later lived as a hermit, a stag would hold Canice's Bible so the man could hold up his hands while he prayed.

KEY VERSE: Rejoice in the LORD, O you righteous! For praise from the upright is beautiful. (Ps. 33:1 NKJV)

Caran (M/F)

MEANING: "pure"

SIGNIFICANCE: Saint Caran of Scotland (died 669) was a missionary bishop.

KEY VERSE: Create in me a pure heart, O God, and renew a steadfast spirit within me. (Ps. 51:10)

Carey (M/F)

MEANING: "from the fortress"

SIGNIFICANCE: William Carey (1761–1834) is considered the father of modern Protestant missions. He spent forty-one years in India, translated the Bible into major Indian languages, and founded a divinity school that still trains students. He is known for living by the phrase "Expect great things from God; attempt great things for God."

KEY VERSE: Since you are my rock and my fortress, for the sake of your name lead and guide me. (Ps. 31:3)

Carlo (SEE CHARLES)

Carmel (M/F)

MEANING: "garden"

SIGNIFICANCE: In the Bible, Mount Carmel was the site of the confrontation between the prophets of Baal and the prophet Elijah. God responded to Elijah's request by sending fire from heaven to show the people that he alone is the Lord.

KEY VERSE: The LORD will guide you continually, giving you water when you are dry and restoring your strength. You will be like a well-watered garden, like an ever-flowing spring. (Isa. 58:11 NLT)

Carmella (SEE CARMEL)

Carmi (M/F)

MEANING: "my vineyard"

SIGNIFICANCE: In the Bible, Carmi was a son of Reuben—Jacob's firstborn.

KEY VERSE: A fine vineyard will appear. There's something to sing about! I, GOD, tend it. I keep it well-watered. I keep careful watch over it. (Isa. 27:2–3 MSG)

Carter (M)

MEANING: "cart driver"

SIGNIFICANCE: Sydney Carter was an English poet, musician, and Quaker Christian best known for his song "Lord of the Dance."

KEY VERSE: You crown the year with your bounty, and your carts overflow with abundance. (Ps. 65:11)

Cassian (M/F)

MEANING: "empty"

SIGNIFICANCE: John Cassian (c. 360–c. 435), a monk in Bethlehem, lived as a hermit and later became a follower of John Chrysostom.

KEY VERSE: The LORD is God, and he created the heavens and earth and put everything in place. He made the world to be lived in, not to be a place of empty chaos. "I am the LORD," he says, "and there is no other." (Isa. 45:18 NLT)

Catherine (F)

MEANING: "pure"

SIGNIFICANCE: Saint Catherine of Sweden (1331–81) and her mother, Saint Bridget, organized pilgrimages to Jerusalem to spur others to spiritual growth. In between pilgrimages, they spent their time in prayer and ministering to the poor.

KEY VERSE: Even a child is known by his actions, by whether his conduct is pure and right. (Prov. 20:11)

Cauvin (SEE CALVIN)

Cecilia (F)

MEANING: "blind"

SIGNIFICANCE: Saint Cecilia (died c. 117) was wed to a pagan nobleman who was so moved by her commitment to God that he became a Christian. The two were eventually martyred for their faith.

KEY VERSE: The LORD opens the eyes of the blind; the LORD raises those who are bowed down; the LORD loves the righteous. (Ps. 146:8 NKJV)

Cedric (M)

MEANING: "amiable"

SIGNIFICANCE: In Sir Walter Scott's *Ivanhoe*, Cedric is the father of the heroine Rowena.

KEY VERSE: Be cheerful.... Keep your spirits up. Think in harmony. Be agreeable. Do all that, and the God of love and peace will be with you for sure. (2 Cor. 13:11 MSG)

Celesta (SEE CELESTE)

C

Celeste (F)

MEANING: "heaven"

SIGNIFICANCE: The name *Celeste* brings to mind images of God's paradise, of his eternal blessing and reward for those who know him.

KEY VERSE: I know that the LORD saves His anointed; He will answer him from His holy heaven with the saving strength of His right hand. (Ps. 20:6 NKJV)

Celestyn (SEE CELESTE)

Celvia (SEE SYLVIA)

Cesario (M)

MEANING: "long-haired"

SIGNIFICANCE: Saint Cesario was a deacon of an African church. On a visit to Italy, he witnessed a pagan celebration of Apollo. When he objected to the human sacrifice involved, he was imprisoned for two years and then martyred.

KEY VERSE: Rise up! Help us! Ransom us because of your unfailing love. (Ps. 44:26 NLT)

Chad (M)

MEANING: "defender"

SIGNIFICANCE: Saint Chad (c. 620–72) founded monasteries, traveled, preached,

reformed monastic life, and built a cathedral on land that had been the site of the martyrdom of a thousand Christians.

KEY VERSE: Let all those rejoice who put their trust in You; let them ever shout for joy, because You defend them; let those also who love Your name be joyful in You. (Ps. 5:11 NKJV)

Chana (SEE FELIX)

Channing (M)

MEANING: "wise"

SIGNIFICANCE: Channing Moore Williams (1829–1910) became bishop of Japan in 1866 and founded St. Paul's University in Tokyo. Later he helped to unite several mission efforts to establish the Roman Catholic Church there.

KEY VERSE: The heart of the discerning acquires knowledge; the ears of the wise seek it out. (Prov. 18:15)

Chantal (F)

MEANING: "song"

SIGNIFICANCE: Saint Jane Frances de Chantel (1572–1641) struggled to forgive the man who had accidentally shot her husband. In time she moved from just greeting him on the street to actually becoming godmother to his child! This experience helped her to open her heart to God and seek to live a more holy life.

KEY VERSE: The LORD is my strength and shield. I trust him with all my heart. He helps me, and my heart is filled with joy. I burst out in songs of thanksgiving. (Ps. 28:7 NLT)

Charity (F)

MEANING: "good will"

SIGNIFICANCE: Saint Charity was a daughter of Saint Sophia and martyred for her faith as a young girl.

KEY VERSE: With good will render service, as to the Lord, and not to men. (Eph. 6:7 NASB)

Charles (M)

MEANING: "strong"

SIGNIFICANCE: As a bishop, Saint Charles Borromeo (1538–84) resolved problems by issuing wise rulings, instituting them with kindness, and setting an example through his own holy life. He learned from having a severe speech impediment that "we are all weak, but if we want help, the Lord God has given us the means to find it easily."

KEY VERSE: Be strong in the Lord and in his mighty power. (Eph. 6:10)

C

Charlotte (F)

MEANING: "little and feminine"

SIGNIFICANCE: Sister Charlotte of the Resurrection (1715–94) was among the group of Carmelite nuns guillotined by the revolutionary French republicans in 1794. As she was thrown to the ground to await her turn, she was heard speaking words of forgiveness and encouragement to her persecutor.

KEY VERSE: How blessed is the man you train, GOD, the woman you instruct in your Word. (Ps. 94:12 MSG)

Cherish (F)

MEANING: "hold dear"

SIGNIFICANCE: To cherish is to nurture or treasure. The Bible says those who cherish God's Word will be blessed.

KEY VERSE: He who cherishes understanding prospers. (Prov. 19:8)

Cherith (F)

MEANING: "separation"

SIGNIFICANCE: In the Bible, the prophet Elijah was miraculously fed by ravens during a time of drought by the brook Cherith.

KEY VERSE: No power in the sky above or in the earth below—indeed, nothing in all creation will ever be able to separate us from the love of God that is revealed in Christ Jesus our Lord. (Rom. 8:39 NLT)

Chiara (SEE CLARE)

Chimone (SEE SIMON)

Chionia (F)

MEANING: "chastity"

SIGNIFICANCE: Saint Chionia (died 304) was convicted of possessing the Scriptures despite being prohibited to do so. When ordered to sacrifice to pagan gods, she refused and was martyred.

KEY VERSE: GOD loves the pure-hearted and well-spoken; good leaders also delight in their friendship. (Prov. 22:11 MSG)

Chloe (F)

MEANING: "fresh blooming"

SIGNIFICANCE: In the Bible, members of Chloe's household informed Paul of dissension in the Corinthian church.

KEY VERSE: As the earth bursts with spring wildflowers, and as a garden cascades with blossoms, so the Master, GOD, brings righteousness into full bloom and puts praise on display before the nations. (Isa. 61:11 MSG)

Chresta (SEE CHRISTIAN)

C

Christao (SEE CHRISTIAN)

Christian (M)

MEANING: "Christ follower"

SIGNIFICANCE: The name *Christian* reflects a commitment to faith in Christ and to following him.

KEY VERSE: [Jesus'] sheep listen to my voice; I know them, and they follow me. (John 10:27)

Christiana (F)

MEANING: "Christ follower"

SIGNIFICANCE: Saint Christiana (seventh century) was an Anglo-Saxon princess who later became a nun.

KEY VERSE: My [Jesus'] sheep listen to my voice; I know them, and they follow me. (John 10:27)

Christino (SEE CHRISTIAN)

Christopher (M)

MEANING: "Christ bearer"

SIGNIFICANCE: The fame of Saint Christopher (died c. 251) comes from a legend in which he bore a small child—whose weight nearly crushed him—across a stream. When he got to the other side, the child said he was Jesus and was so heavy because he bore the weight of the world on himself.

KEY VERSE: Blessed is the man who trusts me, GOD, the woman who sticks with GOD. They're like trees replanted in Eden ... serene and calm through droughts, bearing fresh fruit every season. (Jer. 17:7 MSG)

Chrystek (SEE CHRISTIAN)

Cian (M)

MEANING: "ancient"

SIGNIFICANCE: Saint Cian (sixth century) was a hermit and servant to Saint Peris.

KEY VERSE: I remember your ancient laws, O LORD, and I find comfort in them. (Ps. 119:52)

Ciara (F)

MEANING: "saint"

SIGNIFICANCE: Saint Ciara (died 679) was founder and abbess of a monastery house at Kilkeary, Ireland.

KEY VERSE: Oh, fear the LORD, you His saints! There is no want to those who fear Him. (Ps. 34:9 NKJV)

Cicily (SEE CECILIA)

C

Cillene (F)

MEANING: "cell church"

SIGNIFICANCE: Saint Cillene (died 752) was an elected abbot in Iona, Scotland.

KEY VERSE: The church is Christ's body, in which he speaks and acts, by which he fills everything with his presence. (Eph. 1:23 MSG)

Cisco (SEE FRANCIS)

Clare (F)

MEANING: "bright"

SIGNIFICANCE: Saint Clare of Assisi (1194–1253) was the cofounder of the Poor Clares order, and her love of God, her self-discipline, and her spirit of prayer remain to this day a shining example of devotion.

KEY VERSE: Love flashes like fire, the brightest kind of flame. (Song 8:6 NLT)

Clarissa (SEE CLARE)

Clark (M)

MEANING: "religious person"

SIGNIFICANCE: Explorer William Clark (1770–1838) accompanied Meriwether Lewis on the first US overland expedition to the Pacific coast and back again.

KEY VERSE: Know that the LORD has set apart the godly for himself; the LORD will hear when I call to him. (Ps. 4:3)

Clay (M)

MEANING: "from the earth"

SIGNIFICANCE: In the Bible, Jesus healed a blind man by applying clay to the man's eyes. When the man obeyed Jesus' command to wash his eyes, he could see!

KEY VERSE: O LORD, you are our Father. We are the clay, you are the potter; we are all the work of your hand. (Isa. 64:8)

Clement (M)

·MEANING: "merciful"

SIGNIFICANCE: Clement of Alexandria (c. 170–220) was a theologian and teacher and wrote the first known Christian hymn, "Shepherd of Tender Youth."

KEY VERSE: What does the LORD require of you? To act justly and to love mercy and to walk humbly with your God. (Mic. 6:8)

Cloud (F)

MEANING: "out of the mist"

SIGNIFICANCE: Saint Cloud (522–60) built a monastery near Paris and led a community of monks by his godly example.

KEY VERSE: Your unfailing love, O LORD, is as

vast as the heavens; your faithfulness reaches beyond the clouds. (Ps. 36:5 NLT)

Cole (SEE NICHOLAS)

Colette (F)

MEANING: "victorious army"

SIGNIFICANCE: Saint Colette (1381–1447) was known for her appreciation and care for animals. She was deeply devoted to Christ's Passion and fasted and meditated on it every Friday.

KEY VERSE: Victory comes from you, O LORD. May you bless your people. (Ps. 3:8 NLT)

Collen (M)

MEANING: "handsome"

SIGNIFICANCE: The life of Saint Collen (born c. 600) is shrouded by legend, including tales of his slaying giants and being taken to the land of the faeries, where, as a Christian, he showed the power of God over the old ways.

KEY VERSE: You're the handsomest of men; every word from your lips is sheer grace, and God has blessed you. (Ps. 45:2 MSG)

Colman (M)

MEANING: "dove"

SIGNIFICANCE: Saint Colman of Stockerau (died 1012) was stopped on a pilgrimage to the Holy Land on suspicion of being a spy. With the only evidence against him being that he was a stranger, he was hanged. According to legend, miracles were reported at the site of his death, including the scaffolding taking root and extending branches.

KEY VERSE: Oh that I had wings like a dove; then I would fly away and rest! (Ps. 55:6 NLT)

Columba (M)

MEANING: "dove"

SIGNIFICANCE: Saint Columba (c. 521–97) was an Irish monk, abbot, poet, and founder of monasteries in Britain and Ireland. According to legend, he built his first monastery from stone and rushes so that no tree would have to be cut down, for he didn't want to destroy any of God's creatures.

KEY VERSE: Oh that I had wings like a dove; then I would fly away and rest! (Ps. 55:6 NLT)

Conan (M)

MEANING: "intelligence"

SIGNIFICANCE: Saint Conan of Iona (died 648) was a tutor to princes in Scotland and missionary to the Isle of Man.

KEY VERSE: True intelligence is a spring of fresh water. (Prov. 16:22 MSG)

Conleth (M)

MEANING: "wise"

SIGNIFICANCE: Saint Conleth (c. 450–519) was a skilled goldsmith and manuscript illuminator. He and Saint Brigid ran the first double monastery together.

KEY VERSE: Fear of the LORD is the foundation of true wisdom. All who obey his commandments will grow in wisdom. (Ps. 111:10 NLT)

Conrad (M)

MEANING: "brave counsel"

SIGNIFICANCE: Saint Conrad of Parzham (1818–94) served for more than forty years as a porter, dispensing alms, admitting people to the friary, and encouraging them to open themselves to God.

KEY VERSE: Wait patiently for the LORD. Be brave and courageous. Yes, wait patiently for the LORD. (Ps. 27:14 NLT)

Constance (F)

MEANING: "constancy"

SIGNIFICANCE: Head of the Anglican Community of St. Mary, Constance (died 1878) and her companions were some of the few who stayed to nurse the sick when, in 1878, Memphis was struck by an epidemic of yellow fever that devastated the city.

KEY VERSE: God wants the combination of his steady, constant calling and warm, personal counsel in Scripture to come to characterize us, keeping us alert for whatever he will do next. (Rom. 15:5 MSG)

Constantine (M)

MEANING: "firm"

SIGNIFICANCE: Saint Constantine of Cornwall (died 598) was a king who ceded his throne to his son and became a monk. At the monastery he performed menial tasks for his brothers.

KEY VERSE: The plans of the LORD stand firm forever, the purposes of his heart through all generations. (Ps. 33:11)

Corrie (F)

MEANING: "spear"

SIGNIFICANCE: Corrie ten Boom (1892–1983) was a Dutch Christian who, during World War II, was imprisoned for helping Jews. She was released due to a "clerical error" and spent the rest of her life spreading the message of God's love and forgiveness.

KEY VERSE: Sun and moon stood in their places; they went away at the light of Your arrows, at the radiance of Your gleaming spear. (Hab. 3:11 NASB)

Cotton (M/F)

MEANING: "to unite"

SIGNIFICANCE: Cotton Mather (1663–1728) was a Puritan writer, scholar, and renowned preacher. His *Ecclesiastical History of New*

England remains a landmark of American religious history.

KEY VERSE: Teach me Your way, O LORD; I will walk in Your truth; unite my heart to fear Your name. (Ps. 86:11 NASB)

Craton (M)

MEANING: "from the rocky place"

SIGNIFICANCE: Saint Craton (died c. 273) was a well-known philosopher and converted by Saint Valentine.

KEY VERSE: The LORD is my rock, my fortress and my deliverer; my God is my rock, in whom I take refuge. He is my shield and the horn of my salvation, my stronghold. (Ps. 18:2)

Crispin (M)

MEANING: "curly haired"

SIGNIFICANCE: Saint Crispin (died c. 286) and his brother spread the gospel in Gaul, preaching by day and making shoes by night. Their charity, holy living, and disregard for material things brought many to faith.

KEY VERSE: My life is an example to many, because you have been my strength and protection. (Ps. 71:7 NLT)

Crystal (F)

MEANING: "transparent"

SIGNIFICANCE: The biblical book of Revelation mentions a sea of crystal before the throne of God, as well as a crystal-clear river, flowing with the water of life from the throne and from the Lamb.

KEY VERSE: Train me, GOD, to walk straight; then I'll follow your true path. Put me together, one heart and mind; then, undivided, I'll worship in joyful fear. (Ps. 86:11 MSG)

Cyril (M/F)

MEANING: "ruler"

SIGNIFICANCE: Saint Cyril (827–69) is credited with inventing the Cyrillic alphabet, still used in Russia. He is also noted for insisting on using Slavonic in the Mass, which caused a rift between him and the pope, resulting in the formation of the Greek Orthodox Church.

KEY VERSE: The LORD is in his holy Temple; the LORD still rules from heaven. He watches everyone closely, examining every person on earth. (Ps. 11:4 NLT)

Cyrus (M)

MEANING: "throne"

SIGNIFICANCE: In the Bible, Isaiah referred to Persian king Cyrus as the Lord's anointed. He released the Israelites from captivity and allowed them to rebuild Jerusalem and the temple there.

KEY VERSE: Righteousness and justice are the foundation of Your throne; lovingkindness and truth go before You. (Ps. 89:14 NASB)

"REMEMBER THAT A MAN'S NAME IS, TO
HIM, THE SWEETEST AND MOST IMPORTANT
SOUND IN ANY LANGUAGE."

— DALE CARNEGIE

D

Dacey (SEE CANDACE)

Dag (M)

MEANING: "day"; "brightness"

SIGNIFICANCE: Dag Hammarskjöld (1905–61) served as secretary general of the United Nations from 1953 until his death in a plane crash in 1961. He was known for his wisdom, integrity, modesty, and devotion to God and was awarded the Nobel Peace Prize posthumously.

KEY VERSE: The way of the righteous is like the first gleam of dawn, which shines ever brighter until the full light of day. (Prov. 4:18 NLT)

Daisy (F)

MEANING: "day's eye"

SIGNIFICANCE: Juliette Gordon "Daisy" Low (1860–1927) searched for several years for something meaningful to do with her life. She found it the night she met the man who had founded the Boy Scouts and Girl Guides. Less than a year later, in 1912, she registered eighteen girls in her first troop of Girl Scouts. Membership in the Girls Scouts of the USA now numbers nearly four million.

KEY VERSE: Pay close attention, friend, to what your father tells you; never forget what you learned at your mother's knee. Wear their counsel like flowers in your hair, like rings on your fingers. (Prov. 1:8–9 MSG)

Dallan (M)

MEANING: "blind"

SIGNIFICANCE: Saint Dallan (c. 530–98) went blind as a young man but went on to become the chief bard and poet of Ireland in 575. He is known for helping to preserve the Gaelic language and literature.

KEY VERSE: The LORD opens the eyes of the blind; the LORD raises those who are bowed down; the LORD loves the righteous. (Ps. 146:8 NKJV)

Dalton (M)

MEANING: "from the farm in the dale"

SIGNIFICANCE: John Dalton (1766–1844) is best known for his atomic theory. Of its five main points, three are accepted to this day.

KEY VERSE: Thank you for making me so wonderfully complex! Your workmanship is marvelous—how well I know it. (Ps. 139:14 NLT)

Damaris (F)

MEANING: "gentle girl"

SIGNIFICANCE: Damaris lived in Athens and heard the apostle Paul speak on Mars Hill. As a result of listening to Paul's message, Damaris became a believer.

KEY VERSE: As God's chosen people, holy and dearly loved, clothe yourselves with compassion, kindness, humility, gentleness and patience. (Col. 3:12)

Dan (M)

MEANING: "vindicated"

SIGNIFICANCE: In the Bible, Dan was the fifth son of Jacob.

KEY VERSE: The LORD will vindicate his people and have compassion on his servants. (Ps. 135:14)

Dana (VARIANT OF DANIELLE; SEE DANIEL)

Daniel (M)

MEANING: "God is my judge"

SIGNIFICANCE: In the Bible, Daniel was an Israelite taken in the Babylonian captivity. He was known for his intelligence and his complete loyalty to God. Because of this loyalty, he found himself in a den of lions for disobeying a law that forbade prayer to anyone but the king. God delivered Daniel unharmed.

KEY VERSE: Tell all the nations, "The LORD reigns!" The world stands firm and cannot be shaken. He will judge all peoples fairly. (Ps. 96:10 NLT)

Danielle (SEE DANIEL)

Dannah (M/F)

MEANING: "fortress"

SIGNIFICANCE: In the Bible, Dannah was a town in the Promised Land that was part of the inheritance of the tribe of Judah.

D

Dante (M)

MEANING: "lasting"

SIGNIFICANCE: Dante Alighieri (1265–1321) is best known for his literary masterpiece *The Divine Comedy.*

KEY VERSE: The LORD is good; His lovingkindness is everlasting and His faithfulness to all generations. (Ps. 100:5 NASB)

Dara (F)

MEANING: "pearl"; "marble"

SIGNIFICANCE: In the Bible, Dara was a descendent of Judah, son of Jacob.

KEY VERSE: We, who with unveiled faces all reflect the Lord's glory, are being transformed into his likeness. (2 Cor. 3:18)

Darby (M)

MEANING: "free man"

SIGNIFICANCE: John Nelson Darby (1800–1882) was a British theologian known for his teachings on the end times. His life's philosophy is summed up on his tombstone:
"Lord, let me wait for thee alone; my life be only this: To serve thee here on earth unknown, then share thy heavenly bliss."

KEY VERSE: Oh, thank GOD—he's so good! His love never runs out. All of you set free by GOD, tell the world! (Ps. 107:1–2 MSG)

Darcy (M/F)

MEANING: "from the stronghold"

SIGNIFICANCE: In *Pride and Prejudice*, by Jane Austen, Elizabeth's suitor was named Darcy.

KEY VERSE: He is my loving God and my fortress, my stronghold and my deliverer, my shield, in whom I take refuge, who subdues peoples under me. (Ps. 144:2)

Daria (F)

MEANING: "queenly"

SIGNIFICANCE: Saint Daria (died c. 283) was zealous and public in proclaiming her faith. She was eventually martyred.

KEY VERSE: GOD made the heavens—royal splendor radiates from him, a powerful beauty sets him apart. (Ps. 96:5 MSG)

David (M)

MEANING: "beloved"

SIGNIFICANCE: As a young shepherd, David killed the giant Goliath. He wrote many of the psalms in the Bible and is considered the greatest king Israel has ever known. God himself called David a man after his own heart.

KEY VERSE: Love wisdom like a sister; make insight a beloved member of your family. (Prov. 7:4 NLT)

Dawn (F)

MEANING: "first appearance of light"

SIGNIFICANCE: Dawn is a time for new beginnings, a time when things become clear. Traditionally, it is the moment when a white thread can be distinguished from a black thread.

KEY VERSE: For you who revere my name, the sun of righteousness will rise with healing in its wings. And you will go out and leap like calves released from the stall. (Mal. 4:2)

Dawson (M)

MEANING: "David's son"

SIGNIFICANCE: Dawson Trotman (1906–56) founded the Navigators, a ministry whose motto is "To know Christ and to make Him known."

KEY VERSE: Love wisdom like a sister; make insight a beloved member of your family. (Prov. 7:4 NLT)

Deacon (M)

MEANING: "servant"

SIGNIFICANCE: In the Bible, the first deacons were appointed to assist the apostles with pastoral and administrative tasks.

KEY VERSE: If anyone serves, he should do it with the strength God provides, so that in all things God may be praised. (1 Peter 4:11)

Deborah (F)

MEANING: "bee"

SIGNIFICANCE: In the Bible, Deborah was a judge and wrote the "Song of Deborah," one of the oldest poems in the Bible.

KEY VERSE: Let those who love Him be like the rising of the sun in its might. (Judg. 5:31 NASB)

Declan (M)

MEANING: "famous bearer"

SIGNIFICANCE: Saint Declan discipled early converts of Saint Boniface, helping them to grow stronger in their faith.

KEY VERSE: A good life is a fruit-bearing tree. (Prov. 11:30 MSG)

Dekar (M)

MEANING: "force"

SIGNIFICANCE: In the Bible (1 Kings 4:9 KJV) "the son of Dekar" was one of the governors Solomon appointed to supply provisions for him and his household.

KEY VERSE: The LORD thunders at the head of his army; his forces are beyond number, and mighty are those who obey his command. (Joel 2:11)

Delight (F)

MEANING: "joyful satisfaction"

SIGNIFICANCE: The Bible says that the Lord delights in "uprightness" (1 Chron. 29:17 NASB), in "well-being" (Ps. 35:27), in those who "put their hope in his unfailing love" (Ps. 147:11), in "honesty" (Prov. 11:1 NLT), in "integrity" (Prov. 11:20 NLT), and in "genuine prayers" (Prov. 15:8 MSG).

KEY VERSE: The LORD has done great things for us, and we are filled with joy. (Ps. 126:3)

Delphina (F)

MEANING: "dolphin"

SIGNIFICANCE: Saint Delphina (1283–1360) was a lady to Queen Sanchia in Naples. When the queen died, Delphina sold her vast estates, gave the proceeds to the poor, and lived her remaining years in seclusion.

KEY VERSE: Mightier than the thunder of the great waters, mightier than the breakers of the sea—the LORD on high is mighty. (Ps. 93:4)

Derek (SEE DIETRICH)

DeShawn (SEE DISHON)

Destiny (F)

MEANING: "designated purpose"

SIGNIFICANCE: The word *destiny* comes from an Old French word meaning "to make firm or to establish."

KEY VERSE: "For I know the plans I have for you," declares the LORD, "plans to prosper you and not to harm you, plans to give you hope and a future." (Jer. 29:11)

Devora (SEE DEBORAH)

Diego (M)

MEANING: "supplanter"

SIGNIFICANCE: Saint Diego (1743–1801) was a missionary throughout Spain.

KEY VERSE: I'll give you a new heart, put a new spirit in you. I'll remove the stone heart from your body and replace it with a heart that's God-willed, not self-willed. I'll put my Spirit in you and make it possible for you to do what I tell you and live by my commands. (Ezek. 36:26–27 MSG)

Dietrich (M)

MEANING: "ruler of the people"

SIGNIFICANCE: Dietrich Bonhoeffer (1906–45) was a German pastor and theologian who participated in the resistance movement by rescuing Jews. His belief that being a Christian meant "participation in the sufferings of God" was confirmed when he was incarcerated and later taken to a Nazi prison camp where he was hanged—only one month before Germany's surrender.

KEY VERSE: May the nations be glad and sing for joy, for you rule the peoples justly and guide the nations of the earth. (Ps. 67:4)

Dinah (F)

MEANING: "judgment"

SIGNIFICANCE: In the Bible, Dinah was the lovely daughter of Jacob and Leah.

KEY VERSE: Tell all the nations, "The LORD reigns!" The world stands firm and cannot be shaken. He will judge all peoples fairly. (Ps. 96:10 NLT)

Dion (M)

MEANING: "divine"

SIGNIFICANCE: Dion (408–354 BC) was one of Plato's students.

KEY VERSE: By his divine power, God has given us everything we need for living a godly life. We have received all of this by coming to know him, the one who called us to himself by means of his marvelous glory and excellence. (2 Peter 1:3 NLT)

Dishon (M)

MEANING: "threshing"

SIGNIFICANCE: In the Bible, Dishon was a son of Seir.

KEY VERSE: So let's not get tired of doing what is good. At just the right time we will reap a harvest of blessing if we don't give up. (Gal. 6:9 NLT)

Dixie (SEE BENEDICT)

Dixon (SEE RICHARD)

Dobbs (SEE ROBERT)

Dominic (M)

MEANING: "belonging to God"

SIGNIFICANCE: Saint Dominic Barberi (1792–1849) spent his boyhood as an uneducated shepherd. When he was finally able to attend school, he specialized in philosophy and theology. As a writer, one of his works was based on the idea of integrating science and philosophy. Though condemned at the time, it is now seen as a forerunner of later reforms.

KEY VERSE: You are a chosen people, a royal priesthood, a holy nation, a people belonging to God, that you may declare the praises of him who called you out of darkness into his wonderful light. (1 Peter 2:9)

Dominique (SEE DOMINIC)

Donnan (M)

MEANING: "brown"

SIGNIFICANCE: Saint Donnan (c. seventh century) was a friend and disciple of Saint

Columba. Seeking solitude, Donnan and his friends settled on an island belonging to the queen of Scotland. Upon hearing of this, the queen ordered the men killed.

KEY VERSE: I will lie down and sleep in peace, for you alone, O LORD, make me dwell in safety. (Ps. 4:8)

Dorothea (F)

MEANING: "gift of God"

SIGNIFICANCE: Saint Dorothea (died 311) was martyred during the persecutions of Roman emperor Diocletian. According to legend, Dorothea told the governor who ordered her death that she had remained a virgin because her heart belonged only to Jesus.

KEY VERSE: Children are a gift from the LORD; they are a reward from him. (Ps. 127:3 NLT)

Dorothy (F)

MEANING: "gift of God"

SIGNIFICANCE: Dorothy Sayers (1893–1957) was a Christian mystery writer and apologist. Though writing detective novels was considered outside women's domain, Sayers' intent was not to prove something. She wrote, "The only decent reason for tackling a job is that it is your job, and you want to do it." Several of her "Lord Peter Wimsey" detective novels have become international classics.

KEY VERSE: Children are a gift from the LORD; they are a reward from him. (Ps. 127:3 NLT)

Drew (SEE ANDREW)

Dunstan (M)

MEANING: "from the fortress"

SIGNIFICANCE: Saint Dunstan of Canterbury (909–88) was a monk, expert goldsmith, metalworker, and harpist. He became archbishop of Canterbury in 960.

KEY VERSE: He is my loving God and my fortress, my stronghold and my deliverer, my shield, in whom I take refuge, who subdues peoples under me. (Ps. 144:2)

Dwight (M)

MEANING: "a clearing"

SIGNIFICANCE: Evangelist Dwight L. Moody (1837–99) preached to more than 100 million people during his career. To provide Bible training for laypeople, he began what is now known as the Moody Bible Institute and Moody Press in Chicago. A tireless speaker, he preached six sermons a day just a month before his death.

KEY VERSE: You are God's field, you are God's building. (1 Cor. 3:9 NKJV)

Dylan (M)

MEANING: "of the sea"

SIGNIFICANCE: Dylan Thomas (1914–53) is considered by many to be one of the greatest twentieth-century poets and writers. He is best known for his "A Child's Christmas in Wales" and the now-classic line, "Do not go gentle into that good night."

KEY VERSE: Mightier than the thunder of the great waters, mightier than the breakers of the sea—the LORD on high is mighty. (Ps. 93:4)

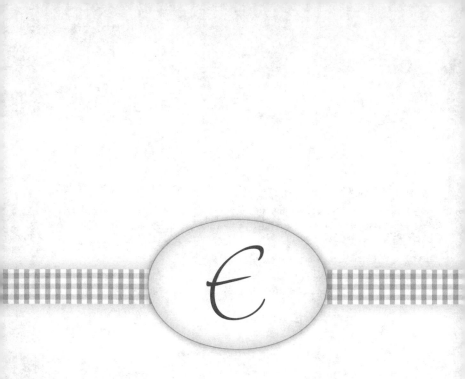

"REMEMBER THAT A MAN'S NAME IS, TO
HIM, THE SWEETEST AND MOST IMPORTANT
SOUND IN ANY LANGUAGE."

— DALE CARNEGIE

Easter (F)

MEANING: "spring"

SIGNIFICANCE: Easter, the celebration of the resurrection of Jesus, is Christendom's most important holy day.

KEY VERSE: Oh, that we might know the LORD! Let us press on to know him! He will respond to us as surely as the arrival of dawn or the coming of rains in early spring. (Hos. 6:3 NLT)

Edana (F)

MEANING: "ardent flame"

SIGNIFICANCE: Saint Edana lived near the rivers Boyle and Shannon. A well is named for her, as are some parishes in Western Ireland. No details of her life have survived.

KEY VERSE: Fire tests the purity of silver and gold, but the LORD tests the heart. (Prov. 17:3 NLT)

Eden (F)

MEANING: "delight"

SIGNIFICANCE: God placed Adam and Eve in the garden of Eden, an environment in which all their needs would be perfectly met.

KEY VERSE: You have made known to me the path of life; you will fill me with joy in your presence. (Ps. 16:11)

Edith (F)

MEANING: "rich bounty"

SIGNIFICANCE: Saint Edith (961–84) was raised in the Wilton abbey and stayed there her entire life. She learned to read, write, and illuminate manuscripts and became a nun at age fifteen.

KEY VERSE: We should make the most of what God gives, both the bounty and the capacity to enjoy it, accepting what's given and delighting in the work. It's God's gift! (Eccl. 5:18 MSG)

Edmund (M)

MEANING: "prosperous protector"

SIGNIFICANCE: Saint Edmund of East Anglia (c. 841–70) was a king who was captured by pagan invaders. The enemy wanted him to sign a treaty that would harm his country and church, but he chose to die rather than to grieve God and hurt his people.

KEY VERSE: For the LORD God is our sun and shield. He gives us grace and glory. The LORD will withhold no good thing from those who do what is right. (Ps. 84:11 NLT)

Edward (M)

MEANING: "happy protector"

SIGNIFICANCE: Saint Edward the Confessor (1003–66) was one of the most popular English kings, because he trusted in God and greatly loved his people. By relying on God, he was able to rule wisely and maintain peace.

KEY VERSE: For the LORD God is our sun and shield. He gives us grace and glory. The LORD will withhold no good thing from those who do what is right. (Ps. 84:11 NLT)

Edwin (M)

MEANING: "prosperous friend"

SIGNIFICANCE: Saint Edwin (585–683) was a pagan king who listened to a Christian preacher publicly explain the gospel. He accepted salvation, renounced his worship of the gods, and commanded his high priest to destroy their altars and temples.

KEY VERSE: Trust in the LORD and do good. Then you will live safely in the land and prosper. (Ps. 37:3 NLT)

Eikki (SEE ERIC)

Ela (M/F)

MEANING: "oak"

SIGNIFICANCE: In the Bible, Ela was the father of Shimei, one of the twelve officers appointed to requisition food for King Solomon's household.

KEY VERSE: You're a tree replanted in Eden, bearing fresh fruit every month, never dropping a leaf, always in blossom. (Ps. 1:2 MSG)

Elam (M)

MEANING: "eternal"

SIGNIFICANCE: In the Bible, Elam was a grandson of Noah.

KEY VERSE: Trust in the LORD forever, for the LORD, the LORD, is the Rock eternal. (Isa. 26:4)

Elana (SEE HELEN)

Eleanor (F)

MEANING: "bright"

SIGNIFICANCE: Eleanor Roosevelt (1884–1962) used her influence as First Lady of the United States to further the causes of both civil and human rights. Harry S. Truman referred to her as "First Lady of the World," acknowledging her passion for and extensive travel on behalf of human rights.

KEY VERSE: Those who are wise will shine like the brightness of the heavens, and those who lead many to righteousness, like the stars for ever and ever. (Dan. 12:3)

Eleazar (M)

MEANING: "God has helped"

SIGNIFICANCE: In the Bible, Eleazar was the third son of Aaron and a high priest after him.

KEY VERSE: Real help comes from GOD. Your blessing clothes your people! (Ps. 3:8 MSG)

Eli (M)

MEANING: "height"

SIGNIFICANCE: In the Bible, Eli was a priest in the sanctuary of the Lord. He heard the prayer of Hannah, and later raised her son Samuel.

KEY VERSE: You, O LORD, are a shield around me; you are my glory, the one who holds my head high. (Ps. 3:3 NLT)

Elian (M)

MEANING: "Jehovah is God"

SIGNIFICANCE: Saint Elian was a sixth-century missionary to Cornwall, England.

KEY VERSE: Our Lord is great, with limitless strength; we'll never comprehend what he knows and does. (Ps. 147:5 MSG)

Elias (M)

MEANING: "Jehovah is God"

SIGNIFICANCE: Saint Elias (died 309), along with four companions, ministered to Christians who were condemned to work the mines of Cilicia during the persecutions of Maximus. His work exposed his faith, which resulted in his execution.

KEY VERSE: Our Lord is great, with limitless strength; we'll never comprehend what he knows and does. (Ps. 147:5 MSG)

$\mathcal{E}$

Elijah (M)

MEANING: "Jehovah is God"

SIGNIFICANCE: In the Bible, Elijah was the prophet who defeated the priests of Baal, restored a dead child to his mother, and appeared with Moses and Jesus in the New Testament transfiguration of Jesus.

KEY VERSE: Know that the LORD is God. It is he who made us, and we are his. (Ps. 100:3)

Elisha (M)

MEANING: "God is salvation"

SIGNIFICANCE: Elisha followed Elijah in prophetic ministry, helping individuals who couldn't help themselves.

KEY VERSE: The LORD is my light and my salvation—whom shall I fear? (Ps. 27:1)

Elisheba (F)

MEANING: "God is my oath"

SIGNIFICANCE: In the Bible, Elisheba was Aaron's wife.

KEY VERSE: The LORD is faithful to all his promises and loving toward all he has made. (Ps. 145:13)

Elissa (SEE ELIZABETH)

Elizabeth (F)

MEANING: "oath of God"

SIGNIFICANCE: In the Bible, Elizabeth was the mother of John the Baptist and a relative of Mary, the mother of Jesus.

KEY VERSE: The LORD is faithful to all his promises and loving toward all he has made. (Ps. 145:13)

E

Elliot (M)

MEANING: "Jehovah is God"

SIGNIFICANCE: Jim Elliot (1927–56) was a missionary to Ecuador who, along with his four associates, was killed by the Huaroni tribe. This event sparked a worldwide interest in and commitment to missions. Elliot's wife, Elisabeth, later wrote a book chronicling the ministries and deaths of Jim and the other four missionaries called *Through Gates of Splendor.* Elliot is noted for his statement "He is no fool who gives what he cannot keep to gain what he cannot lose."

KEY VERSE: Our Lord is great, with limitless strength; we'll never comprehend what he knows and does. (Ps. 147:5 MSG)

Elona (SEE HELEN)

Elvan (M)

MEANING: "wise friend"

SIGNIFICANCE: Saint Elvan (second century) was sent by his king to the pope to request that missionaries be sent to Britain.

KEY VERSE: The LORD is a friend to those who fear him. He teaches them his covenant. (Ps. 25:14 NLT)

Emerson (M)

MEANING: "son of the industrious ruler"

SIGNIFICANCE: Ralph Waldo Emerson (1803–82) was an American author and poet best known for his essays and the poem "Concord Hymn," in which he originated the phrase "the shot heard round the world."

KEY VERSE: May the nations be glad and sing for joy, for you rule the peoples justly and guide the nations of the earth. (Ps. 67:4)

E

Emilian (M)

MEANING: "eager"

SIGNIFICANCE: Saint Emilian (died 259) was a soldier who was martyred for his faith.

KEY VERSE: How exquisite your love, O God! How eager we are to run under your wings.... You're a fountain of cascading light, and you open our eyes to light. (Ps. 36:7, 9 MSG)

Emiliana (F)

MEANING: "eager"

SIGNIFICANCE: According to legend, Saint Emiliana spent so much time kneeling in prayer that her knees and elbows became locked arthritically in that position.

KEY VERSE: How exquisite your love, O God! How eager we are to run under your wings.... You're a fountain of cascading light, and you open our eyes to light. (Ps. 36:7, 9 MSG)

Emilina (F)

MEANING: "industrious"

SIGNIFICANCE: Saint Emilina (115–78) was noted for her deep prayer life, fasts, and self-imposed penances. When word of her devotion spread, pilgrims came to consult with her about holiness and prayer. She never sought honor for herself, but dealt with visitors humbly and patiently, always concerned with their relationship with God.

KEY VERSE: Turn away from evil and do good. Search for peace, and work to maintain it. (Ps. 34:14 NLT)

Emma (F)

MEANING: "whole"

$\mathcal{E}$

SIGNIFICANCE: Queen Emma of Hawaii (1836–85) was, along with her husband, interested in spreading Christianity and encouraged the building of Christian schools and hospitals in her country. Her husband also translated both the *Anglican Book of Common Prayer* and much of the Anglican hymnal into Hawaiian.

KEY VERSE: So you'll go out in joy, you'll be led into a whole and complete life. The mountains and hills will lead the parade, bursting with song. All the trees of the forest will join the procession, exuberant with applause. (Isa. 55:12 MSG)

Emmanuel (M)

MEANING: "consecrated"

SIGNIFICANCE: The statement in Matthew 1:23, "The virgin will be with child and will give birth to a son, and they will call him Immanuel— which means, 'God with us,'" is a reference to a prophecy made by Isaiah (7:14).

KEY VERSE: Know that the LORD has set apart the godly for himself; the LORD will hear when I call to him. (Ps. 4:3)

Enoch (M)

MEANING: "dedicated"

SIGNIFICANCE: In the Bible, Enoch is said to have been so close to God that he didn't experience death: God simply took him to heaven.

KEY VERSE: Commit everything you do to the LORD. Trust him, and he will help you. (Ps. 37:5 NLT)

Ephraim (M)

MEANING: "very fruitful"

SIGNIFICANCE: In the Bible, Ephraim was the younger son of Joseph.

KEY VERSE: From the fruit of his lips a man is filled with good things as surely as the work of his hands rewards him. (Prov. 12:14)

Eran (M)

MEANING: "peace"

SIGNIFICANCE: In the Old Testament, Eran was a great-grandson of Joseph.

KEY VERSE: The LORD gives strength to his people; the LORD blesses his people with peace. (Ps. 29:11)

Eric (M)

MEANING: "ever powerful"

SIGNIFICANCE: King Eric of Sweden (died 1161) used his throne to spread the gospel throughout his kingdom and zealously defended both his country and his faith.

KEY VERSE: Great is our Lord and mighty in power; his understanding has no limit. (Ps. 147:5)

Esdra (SEE EZRA)

Esevan (SEE STEPHEN)

Essias (SEE ISAIAH)

Esther (F)

MEANING: "star"

SIGNIFICANCE: In the Bible Esther was the Jewish queen of King Xerxes of Persia. She risked her life to approach the king to ask him to spare her people from a massacre orchestrated by one of his officials. Her success is remembered each year at the Jewish Feast of Purim.

E

KEY VERSE: Those who are wise will shine like the brightness of the heavens, and those who lead many to righteousness, like the stars for ever and ever. (Dan. 12:3)

Ethan (M)

MEANING: "firm"

SIGNIFICANCE: In the Bible Ethan was a descendent of Levi and one of three outstanding musicians appointed by David. He is likely the "chief Musician" referred to in the title to Psalm 39 KJV and probably composed the music for it.

KEY VERSE: If the LORD delights in a man's way, he makes his steps firm; though he stumble, he will not fall, for the LORD upholds him with his hand. (Ps. 37:23–24)

Eunice (F)

MEANING: "good victory"

SIGNIFICANCE: In the Bible, Eunice was a Jewish Christian and the mother of Timothy, to whom she taught the Old Testament Scriptures from the time he was very young.

KEY VERSE: Everyone runs; one wins. Run to win. (1 Cor. 9:24 MSG)

Evan (M)

MEANING: "young warrior"

SIGNIFICANCE: Saint Evan (ninth century) made pilgrimages both to Rome and Jerusalem and later became a hermit at Ayrshire, Scotland, where a church is built on what is thought to be his cell.

KEY VERSE: Praise be to the LORD my Rock, who trains my hands for war, my fingers for battle. (Ps. 144:1)

E

Eve (F)

MEANING: "life"

SIGNIFICANCE: Eve was the first woman created by God.

KEY VERSE: Now you've got my feet on the life path, all radiant from the shining of your face. Ever since you took my hand, I'm on the right way. (Ps. 16:11 MSG)

Evelyn (F)

MEANING: "life"

SIGNIFICANCE: Evelyn Underhill (1850–1941) lived a life of reading, writing, meditation, and prayer. She wrote several books on contemplative prayer and taught that it was a practice accessible to any Christian willing to undertake it.

KEY VERSE: Now you've got my feet on the life path, all radiant from the shining of your face. Ever since you took my hand, I'm on the right way. (Ps. 16:11 MSG)

Ezekiel (M)

MEANING: "strength of God"

SIGNIFICANCE: Ezekiel was a prophet who served God during Israel's captivity in Babylon. He received vivid visions from God and delivered difficult messages fearlessly.

KEY VERSE: The LORD is my strength and my shield; my heart trusts in him, and I am helped. (Ps. 28:7)

Ezra (M)

MEANING: "helper"

SIGNIFICANCE: Ezra led the second group of exiles from Babylon back to Jerusalem and may have been the author of 1 and 2 Chronicles.

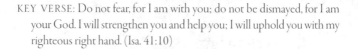

KEY VERSE: Do not fear, for I am with you; do not be dismayed, for I am your God. I will strengthen you and help you; I will uphold you with my righteous right hand. (Isa. 41:10)

F

"REMEMBER THAT A MAN'S
NAME IS, TO HIM, THE
SWEETEST AND MOST
IMPORTANT SOUND IN ANY
LANGUAGE."

— DALE CARNEGIE

F

Fabian (M)

MEANING: "bean grower"

SIGNIFICANCE: Pope Fabian (died 250) was a farmer who went to Rome on a day when a new pope was to be elected. A dove flew down and settled on his head, and those gathered there took it as a sign that Fabian had been anointed. He was chosen pope by acclamation.

KEY VERSE: I'm an olive tree, growing green in God's house. I trusted in the generous mercy of God then and now. (Ps. 52:8 MSG)

Faith (F)

MEANING: "loyalty"; "belief"

SIGNIFICANCE: First Corinthians 13:13 names faith as one of the three most important virtues: faith, hope, and love.

KEY VERSE: The word of the LORD is right and true; he is faithful in all he does. (Ps. 33:4)

Fania (SEE FRANCIS)

Fanny (F)

MEANING: "free"

SIGNIFICANCE: Throughout her long career, Fanny Crosby (1820–1915) wrote more than 8,500 hymns, including "Blessed Assurance," "Near the Cross," and "Redeemed, How I Love to Proclaim It!" Blind from infancy as a result of incorrect medical treatment,

Fanny learned the Bible with a passion—memorizing most of the New Testament and more than five books of the Old Testament by the time she was ten.

KEY VERSE: I run in the path of your commands, for you have set my heart free. (Ps. 119:32)

Faris (M/F)

MEANING: "iron"

SIGNIFICANCE: John T. Faris was a friend of clergyman and best-selling devotional writer James Russell Miller. Upon Miller's death, Faris completed Miller's unfinished final manuscript and published it as *The Book of Comfort.*

KEY VERSE: Invigorate my soul so I can praise you well, use your decrees to put iron in my soul. (Ps. 119:175 MSG)

Faro (M)

MEANING: "headlight"

SIGNIFICANCE: Saint Faro (died 675) was a bishop who worked for renewal in monastic life and was known for his charity to the poor.

KEY VERSE: The LORD is my light and my salvation— whom shall I fear? The LORD is the stronghold of my life—of whom shall I be afraid? (Ps. 27:1)

F

Felice (F)

MEANING: "happy"

SIGNIFICANCE: Saint Felice da Nicosia (1715–87) tried to enter a convent for eight years before he was finally admitted. He worked tirelessly with the sick during a plague and came through unharmed. He was so devoted to his order that he asked permission to die.

KEY VERSE: O LORD of Heaven's Armies, what joy for those who trust in you. (Ps. 84:12 NLT)

Felicitas (F)

MEANING: "happy"

SIGNIFICANCE: Saint Felicitas (died 203) was a maid, friend, and fellow convert with Saint Perpetua. They were martyred together, and their story became so popular that Saint Augustine warned against giving it the weight of Scripture.

KEY VERSE: Joyful are people of integrity, who follow the instructions of the LORD. (Ps. 119:1 NLT)

Felicity (F)

MEANING: "happy"

SIGNIFICANCE: Saint Felicity (died 165) was devoted to charity and caring for the poor. She was martyred for refusing to worship pagan gods.

KEY VERSE: Those who listen to instruction will prosper; those who trust the LORD will be joyful. (Prov. 16:20 NLT)

Felix (M)

MEANING: "fortunate"

SIGNIFICANCE: Saint Felix (died c. 303) was ordered to offer sacrifices to pagan gods. When he refused and prayed instead, the idols shattered.

KEY VERSE: Open your mouth and taste, open your eyes and see—how good GOD is. Blessed are you who run to him. (Ps. 34:8 MSG)

Finden (M)

MEANING: "judge"

SIGNIFICANCE: Saint Finden (c. 470–c. 550) is considered one of the great founders of Irish monasticism. He founded the monastery at Clonard, Meath, Ireland, that lasted for a thousand years.

KEY VERSE: Tell all the nations, "The LORD reigns!" The world stands firm and cannot be shaken. He will judge all peoples fairly. (Ps. 96:10 NLT)

Finnian (M)

MEANING: "fair"; "light"

SIGNIFICANCE: Saint Finnian of Moville (c. 495–589) was a bishop who founded both a school and a monastery and was a spiritual teacher of Saint Columba.

KEY VERSE: The LORD is my light and my salvation—whom shall I fear? The LORD is the stronghold of my life—of whom shall I be afraid? (Ps. 27:1)

Fisher (M)

MEANING: "one who fishes"

SIGNIFICANCE: Jesus' call to Peter and Andrew sums up his call to all believers everywhere—to be a "fisher of men" is to share God's love with everyone.

KEY VERSE: "Come, follow me," Jesus said, "and I will make you fishers of men." (Matt. 4:19)

Flavian (M)

MEANING: "yellow-haired"

SIGNIFICANCE: When the people of Carthage revolted against the Roman emperor, the local government blamed the Christians. Saint Flavian (died 259) was one of several martyrs in the region at that time.

KEY VERSE: God blesses those who patiently endure testing and temptation. Afterward they will receive the crown of life that God has promised to those who love him. (James 1:12 NLT)

F

Flora (F)

MEANING: "flower"

SIGNIFICANCE: Saint Flora of Kildare (died 523) was a cook in the convent of Saint Brigid. She is remembered for her simple, personal godliness.

KEY VERSE: If God cares so wonderfully for wildflowers that are here today and thrown into the fire tomorrow, he will certainly care for you. (Matt. 6:30 NLT)

Francis (M/F)

MEANING: "free"

SIGNIFICANCE: When Saint Francis of Assisi (1181–1226) came to faith, his father disinherited him. He served the sick, preached in the streets, worked with his hands, cared for lepers, and sent food to thieves. His well-known prayer that begins "Lord, make me an instrument of Thy peace" sums up the way Saint Francis lived.

KEY VERSE: I run in the path of your commands, for you have set my heart free. (Ps. 119:32)

Francisca (F)

MEANING: "free"

SIGNIFICANCE: Saint Francisca (1844–1915) founded, with her father, an order dedicated to helping the young women who were pouring into the cities during the Industrial Revolution. She also opened homes and schools for working-class girls.

KEY VERSE: I run in the path of your commands, for you have set my heart free. (Ps. 119:32)

Franklin (M)

MEANING: "free landowner"

SIGNIFICANCE: Benjamin Franklin (1706–1790) was a noted printer, scientist, inventor, and activist. His diplomatic work during the American Revolution secured the help of the French, making independence possible.

KEY VERSE: I run in the path of your commands, for you have set my heart free. (Ps. 119:32)

Freda (F)

MEANING: "peaceful"

SIGNIFICANCE: Upon her husband's death, Freda Lindsey (1916–) took the helm of their fledgling school for training theologians and proceeded to oversee the building of an eighty-acre debt-free campus. In the decades that followed she raised 100 million dollars for missions, launched thirty Bible colleges worldwide, and established 11,000 churches.

KEY VERSE: How beautiful on the mountains are the feet of those who bring good news, who proclaim peace, who bring good tidings. (Isa. 52:7)

Fulton (M)

MEANING: "field town"

SIGNIFICANCE: Robert Fulton (1765–1815) was an American inventor who patented many inventions, including the steamboat.

KEY VERSE: You are God's field, you are God's building. (1 Cor. 3:9 NKJV)

G

"REMEMBER THAT A MAN'S NAME IS, TO HIM, THE SWEETEST AND MOST IMPORTANT SOUND IN ANY LANGUAGE."

— DALE CARNEGIE

G

Gabriel (M)

MEANING: "strength of God"

SIGNIFICANCE: In the Bible, Gabriel was the angel of God who appeared to Mary, the mother of Jesus, to tell her she would give birth to God's Son.

KEY VERSE: Do not fear, for I am with you; do not be dismayed, for I am your God. I will strengthen you and help you; I will uphold you with my righteous right hand. (Isa. 41:10)

Garland (M/F)

MEANING: "wreath"

SIGNIFICANCE: The first European settlers in America brought with them the tradition of Christmas garlands. Using pine, holly, cedar blueberries, myrtle, bittersweet pods, and other natural materials, people wove their decorations and often sold them to buy clothing or gifts.

KEY VERSE: [Wisdom] will set a garland of grace on your head and present you with a crown of splendor. (Prov. 4:9)

Garrett (SEE GERARD)

Garrison (M)

MEANING: "spear-fortified town"

SIGNIFICANCE: William Lloyd Garrison (1805–79) was an abolitionist, journalist, editor of *The Liberator* (a radical abolitionist newspaper), and one of the founders of the American Anti-Slavery Society.

KEY VERSE: Sun and moon stood in their places; they went away at the light of Your arrows, at the radiance of Your gleaming spear. (Hab. 3:11 NASB)

Gavin (M)

MEANING: "little hawk"

SIGNIFICANCE: Gavin (Gawain) was the first knight of King Arthur's Round Table.

KEY VERSE: Look at the birds. They don't need to plant or harvest or store food in barns, for your heavenly Father feeds them. And aren't you far more valuable to him than they are? (Matt 6:26 NLT)

Gemma (F)

MEANING: "jewel"

SIGNIFICANCE: Saint Gemma (died 1249) was a shepherdess and recluse.

KEY VERSE: Lips that speak knowledge are a rare jewel. (Prov. 20:15)

Genevieve (F)

MEANING: "white wave"

SIGNIFICANCE: Saint Genevieve (422–500) was a small child when she decided to devote

G

her life to God. She allowed nothing to interfere. She had an enthusiastic and single-minded heart for Christ.

KEY VERSE: All who are victorious will be clothed in white. I will never erase their names from the Book of Life, but I will announce before my Father and his angels that they are mine. (Rev. 3:5 NLT)

Geoffrey (M)

MEANING: "heavenly peace"

SIGNIFICANCE: Geoffrey Chaucer (c. 1343–1400) is often referred to as the Father of English Literature and is best known for his *Canterbury Tales*.

KEY VERSE: The LORD gives strength to his people; the LORD blesses his people with peace. (Ps. 29:11)

George (M)

MEANING: "farmer"

SIGNIFICANCE: Saint George (died c. 304) is the subject of many legends. According to the "Golden Legend," he killed a dragon that had been regularly attacking several villages. When the king gave him a large reward, he distributed it among the poor and rode away.

KEY VERSE: So let's not get tired of doing what is good. At just the right time we will reap a harvest of blessing if we don't give up. (Gal. 6:9 NLT)

G

Georgia (F)

MEANING: "farmer"

SIGNIFICANCE: Georgia Harkness (1891–1974) is considered one of the first significant American female theologians and was also one of the first women to teach in a seminary.

KEY VERSE: So let's not get tired of doing what is good. At just the right time we will reap a harvest of blessing if we don't give up.. (Gal. 6:9 NLT)

Gerald (M)

MEANING: "spear ruler"

SIGNIFICANCE: Saint Gerald (died 1109) was a choir director of the Cathedral of Toledo who was called to help in spreading reform in Spain. He became such an influence for good that the people and clergy of the city of Braga selected him to be their bishop.

KEY VERSE: May the nations be glad and sing for joy, for you rule the peoples justly and guide the nations of the earth. (Ps. 67:4)

Gerard (M)

MEANING: "spear strong"

SIGNIFICANCE: Saint Gerard (died 1138) was the brother and closest confidant of Bernard of Clairvaux.

KEY VERSE: Sun and moon stood in their places;

they went away at the light of Your arrows, at the radiance of Your gleaming spear. (Hab. 3:11 NASB)

Gerek (SEE GERARD)

Gereon (M)

MEANING: "old"

SIGNIFICANCE: Saint Gereon (died c. 304) was a Roman soldier who was martyred with several others when he refused to obey the emperor's order to sacrifice to pagan gods in order to obtain victory in battle.

KEY VERSE: Remember, O LORD, your great mercy and love, for they are from of old. (Ps. 25:6)

Germaine (M)

MEANING: "loud of voice"

SIGNIFICANCE: Saint Germaine Cousin (1579–1601) was severely abused and neglected as a child but turned to God to learn to forgive and grow in holiness. As a shepherdess, she left her sheep in God's care daily when she went to pray.

KEY VERSE: Sing praises to God and to his name! Sing loud praises to him who rides the clouds. His name is the LORD—rejoice in his presence! (Ps. 68:4 NLT)

Giah (F)

MEANING: "to guide"

SIGNIFICANCE: In the Bible, Giah is a place near Gibeon.

KEY VERSE: If I rise on the wings of the dawn, if I settle on the far side of the sea, even there your hand will guide me, your right hand will hold me fast. (Ps. 139:9–10)

Gian (SEE JOHN)

Gibrian (M)

MEANING: "aristocrat"

SIGNIFICANCE: Saint Gibrian (died c. 515) was the eldest of ten siblings and determined to spend his life in communion with God. He spent his adult life in prayer and self-denial as a hermit, acting as spiritual leader to his brothers and sisters who all lived nearby.

KEY VERSE: The noble man makes noble plans, and by noble deeds he stands. (Isa. 32:8)

Gideon (M)

MEANING: "destroyer"

SIGNIFICANCE: In the Bible, Gideon was a judge of Israel and led a very small army to defeat the vast forces of the Midianites.

G

Gilbert (M)

MEANING: "trusted"

SIGNIFICANCE: Saint Gilbert (died 1245) was a Scottish bishop and fierce proponent of Scottish independence, willing even to oppose the archbishop of York in matters that might threaten that independence.

KEY VERSE: Those who know your name will trust in you, for you, LORD, have never forsaken those who seek you. (Ps. 9:10)

Giles (M)

MEANING: "shield bearer"

SIGNIFICANCE: Saint Giles of Assisi (died 1263) was one of Saint Francis's earliest followers. Though known for his austerity and silence, his "Golden Sayings of Brother Francis" is noted for its humor, deep understanding of human nature, and optimism.

KEY VERSE: You, O LORD, are a shield around me; you are my glory, the one who holds my head high. (Ps. 3:3 NLT)

Gillian (SEE JULIAN)

Giotto (M)

MEANING: "God's peace"

SIGNIFICANCE: Giotto (1267–1337) was an Italian painter and architect who is considered the first of the artists who contributed to the Italian Renaissance. He is known for infusing human emotion into the subjects of his paintings.

KEY VERSE: The LORD gives strength to his people; the LORD blesses his people with peace. (Ps. 29:11)

Gisella (F)

MEANING: "pledge"

SIGNIFICANCE: Saint Gisella (died c. 1095), the first queen of Hungary, used her position for charitable work and retired to a convent after her husband's death.

KEY VERSE: I have taken an oath and confirmed it, that I will follow your righteous laws. (Ps. 119:106)

Glory (F)

MEANING: "renown"

SIGNIFICANCE: The glory of God is a manifestation of his presence and also a description of his magnificence.

KEY VERSE: The LORD God is a sun and shield; the LORD bestows favor and honor; no good thing does he withhold from those whose walk is blameless. (Ps. 84:11)

Grace (F)

MEANING: "favor"

SIGNIFICANCE: Divine grace is God's favor and mercy bestowed on humanity.

KEY VERSE: God is able to make all grace abound to you, so that in all things at all times, having all that you need, you will abound in every good work. (2 Cor. 9:8)

Gracia (F)

MEANING: "graceful"

SIGNIFICANCE: Saint Gracia (died c. 1180) was a sister to Saint Bernard, who brought her to faith. When they shared their faith with another brother, he turned them over to the authorities, who martyred them.

KEY VERSE: Praise the LORD, for the LORD is good; sing praises to His name, for it is lovely. (Ps. 135:3 NASB)

Gracian (M)

MEANING: "favor"

SIGNIFICANCE: Baltasar Gracian (1601–58), a Spanish Jesuit writer, is best known for his work *The Art of Worldly Wisdom*, a compilation of advice for success in the world.

KEY VERSE: God is able to make all grace abound to you, so that in all things at all times, having all that you need, you will abound in every good work. (2 Cor. 9:8)

Graecina (F)

MEANING: "favor"

SIGNIFICANCE: Saint Graecina (died fourth

century) was martyred in the persecutions of Emperor Diocletian. No other information is known.

KEY VERSE: God is able to make all grace abound to you, so that in all things at all times, having all that you need, you will abound in every good work. (2 Cor. 9:8)

Graham (M)

MEANING: "warring"

SIGNIFICANCE: Evangelist Billy Graham (1918–) has preached in person to more than eighty million people. His message has remained the same over the years, and he says, "Christians are not limited to any church. The only question is, Are you committed to Christ?"

KEY VERSE: Praise be to the LORD my Rock, who trains my hands for war, my fingers for battle. (Ps. 144:1)

Grant (M)

MEANING: "great"

SIGNIFICANCE: Ulysses S. Grant (1822–85) was the commander of the Union Army during the Civil War and later president of the United States.

KEY VERSE: You are great and do marvelous deeds; you alone are God. (Ps. 86:10)

Gregor (M)

MEANING: "watchful"

SIGNIFICANCE: Gregor Mendel (1822–84) is often called the "father of genetics" for his study of the inheritance of traits in pea plants.

KEY VERSE: Make sure you stay alert. Keep close watch over yourselves. Don't forget anything of what you've seen. Don't let your heart wander off. Stay vigilant as long as you live. (Deut. 4:9 MSG)

Gregory (M)

MEANING: "watchful"

SIGNIFICANCE: Gregory the Great (c. 540–604) was the first monk ever to be named pope. He collected the melodies and plain chants so associated with him that they are now known as "Gregorian Chants."

KEY VERSE: Make sure you stay alert. Keep close watch over yourselves. Don't forget anything of what you've seen. Don't let your heart wander off. Stay vigilant as long as you live. (Deut. 4:9 MSG)

Griffin (M)

MEANING: "strong in faith"

SIGNIFICANCE: The griffin (or gryphon) is a mythological creature with the body of a lion and the head and wings of an eagle. Because the lion was considered the king of the beasts and the eagle the king of the air, the griffin was thought to be especially strong and majestic.

KEY VERSE: Watch, stand fast in the faith, be brave, be strong. (1 Cor. 16:13 NKJV)

Gustin (SEE JUSTIN)

Gwendoline (F)

MEANING: "white"

SIGNIFICANCE: Saint Gwendoline (died c. 750) was a daughter of a duke and a Benedictine nun.

KEY VERSE: All who are victorious will be clothed in white. I will never erase their names from the Book of Life, but I will announce before my Father and his angels that they are mine. (Rev. 3:5 NLT)

Gwinear (M/F)

MEANING: unknown

SIGNIFICANCE: Saint Gwinear (died c. 460) came to faith when Saint Patrick visited Gwinear's father, the king of Ireland.

KEY VERSE: Open your mouth and taste, open your eyes and see—how good GOD is. Blessed are you who run to him. (Ps. 34:8 MSG)

Gwynne (F)

MEANING: "white'

SIGNIFICANCE: Sarah Gwynne (1746–1842) was the wife of Charles Wesley and was known for her lovely singing voice.

G

KEY VERSE: All who are victorious will be clothed in white. I will never erase their names from the Book of Life, but I will announce before my Father and his angels that they are mine. (Rev. 3:5 NLT)

H

"REMEMBER THAT A MAN'S NAME IS, TO
HIM, THE SWEETEST AND MOST IMPORTANT
SOUND IN ANY LANGUAGE."

— DALE CARNEGIE

H

Halina (SEE HELEN)

Hank (SEE HENRY)

Hannah (F)

MEANING: "graceful"

SIGNIFICANCE: In the Bible, Hannah was the mother of Samuel, the greatest and last judge of Israel.

KEY VERSE: He makes my feet like the feet of a deer; he enables me to stand on the heights. (Ps. 18:33)

Hans (M)

MEANING: "God is gracious"

SIGNIFICANCE: Hans Wilhelm Frei (1922–88) was a theologian best known for his books *The Eclipse of Biblical Narrative* and *The Identity of Jesus Christ.*

KEY VERSE: The LORD is compassionate and gracious, slow to anger, abounding in love. (Ps. 103:8)

Harmony (F)

MEANING: "tranquility"

SIGNIFICANCE: Harmony is one of the most elusive yet beautiful sounds—perfect unity.

KEY VERSE: Mercy, peace and love be yours in abundance. (Jude 1:2)

H

Haroun (SEE AARON)

Harriet (F)

> MEANING: "ruler of the home"

> SIGNIFICANCE: Harriet Beecher Stowe (1811–96) was an abolitionist and author, best known for her book *Uncle Tom's Cabin,* the first major American novel with an African-American hero.

> KEY VERSE: May the nations be glad and sing for joy, for you rule the peoples justly and guide the nations of the earth. (Ps. 67:4)

Harry (M)

> MEANING: "soldier"

> SIGNIFICANCE: Harry Ironside (1876–1951) was an American Bible teacher, pastor of Moody Memorial Church in Chicago, and author of more than sixty works.

> KEY VERSE: Praise be to the LORD my Rock, who trains my hands for war, my fingers for battle. (Ps. 144:1)

Heidi (F)

> MEANING: "noble rank"

> SIGNIFICANCE: The book *Heidi* by Johanna Spyri features the young girl Heidi who is forced into moving from the Swiss Alps to the city, where she learns to read, handle change, and help others.

H

KEY VERSE: The noble man makes noble plans, and by noble deeds he stands. (Isa. 32:8)

Helah (F)

MEANING: "rust"

SIGNIFICANCE: In the Bible, Helah was a wife of Ashur.

KEY VERSE: If I speak with human eloquence and angelic ecstasy but don't love, I'm nothing but the creaking of a rusty gate. (1 Cor. 13:1 MSG)

Helaine (SEE HELEN)

Helen (F)

MEANING: "light"

SIGNIFICANCE: Saint Helen Duglioli (1472–1520) was married against her will but spent thirty happy years with her husband. Upon his death, she devoted herself to charity.

KEY VERSE: The LORD is my light and my salvation—whom shall I fear? The LORD is the stronghold of my life—of whom shall I be afraid? (Ps. 27:1)

Helena (F)

MEANING: "light"

SIGNIFICANCE: Saint Helena (250–330) was married to the coregent of the western Roman Empire and used her position and wealth in the service of her religious enthusiasm and helped to build churches throughout the empire.

KEY VERSE: The LORD is my light and my salvation—whom shall I fear? The LORD is the stronghold of my life—of whom shall I be afraid? (Ps. 27:1)

Henrietta (F)

MEANING: "mistress of the household"

SIGNIFICANCE: Henrietta Mears' (1890–1963) unwavering passion for communicating God's Word began at age twelve when she taught her first Sunday school class. She spent her life educating young people and founded Gospel Light Communications, including an international division.

KEY VERSE: While we have opportunity, let us do good to all people, and especially to those who are of the household of the faith. (Gal. 6:10 NASB)

Henry (M)

MEANING: "ruler of an estate"

SIGNIFICANCE: O. Henry was the pen name of author William Sydney Porter (1862–1910) who was best known for the twists he put on the endings to his short stories, the most famous of which is "The Gift of the Magi."

KEY VERSE: May the nations be glad and sing for joy, for you rule the peoples justly and guide the nations of the earth. (Ps. 67:4)

Heron (M/F)

MEANING: "high"

SIGNIFICANCE: Saint Heron (died c. 136) was the spiritual student of Saint Ignatius and bishop of Antioch for twenty years.

KEY VERSE: You, O LORD, are a shield around me; you are my glory, the one who holds my head high. (Ps. 3:3 NLT)

Hewett (SEE HUGH)

Hilary (F)

MEANING: "merry"

SIGNIFICANCE: Saint Hilary of Poitiers (315–68) is known for her avid defense of Jesus' divinity.

KEY VERSE: May the righteous be glad and rejoice before God; may they be happy and joyful. (Ps. 68:3)

Hilda (F)

MEANING: "woman warrior"

SIGNIFICANCE: Saint Hilda (614–80) served as abbess of a double monastery and was known for her spiritual wisdom.

KEY VERSE: Praise be to the LORD my Rock, who trains my hands for war, my fingers for battle. (Ps. 144:1)

Hob (SEE ALBERT)

Hodia (M/F)

MEANING: "praise the Lord"

KEY VERSE: Praise the Lord; praise God our savior! For each day he carries us in his arms. (Ps. 68:19 NLT)

Honey (F)

MEANING: "sweet"

KEY VERSE: Kind words are like honey—sweet to the soul and healthy for the body. (Prov. 16:24 NLT)

Honor (F)

MEANING: "integrity"

KEY VERSE: Blessed are the pure in heart, for they will see God. (Matt. 5:8)

Hood (M)

MEANING: "strong ruler" (variant of Richard)

SIGNIFICANCE: Robin Hood is a legendary outlaw folk hero known in modern tales as one who fought injustice and tyranny and took from the rich to give to the poor.

KEY VERSE: May the nations be glad and sing for joy, for you rule the peoples justly and guide the nations of the earth. (Ps. 67:4)

Hope (F)

MEANING: "expect with confidence"

KEY VERSE: May your unfailing love rest upon us, O LORD, even as we put our hope in you. (Ps. 33:22)

Hosanna (F)

MEANING: "save"; "preserve"; "keep"

SIGNIFICANCE: As Jesus rode into Jerusalem just a few days before he was crucified, the people lined the streets, shouting, "Hosanna! Blessed is he who comes in the name of the Lord!" (John 12:13).

KEY VERSE: Keep me as the apple of Your eye; hide me under the shadow of Your wings. (Ps. 17:8 NKJV)

Howe (SEE HUGH)

Hudson (M)

MEANING: "son of the hooded man"

SIGNIFICANCE: Hudson Taylor (1832–1905) was a missionary to China known for his zeal for the gospel and the then-radical idea of wearing Chinese clothing and hairstyle. The mission he founded in 1865 continues to operate today.

KEY VERSE: How great is the love the Father has lavished on us, that we should be called children of God! And that is what we are! (1 John 3:1)

Hugh (M)

MEANING: "intelligent"

SIGNIFICANCE: Saint Hugh (c. 1135–1200),

bishop of Lincoln, was known for his generosity and integrity. He raised the quality of education at the cathedral school, and, when Lincoln Cathedral was badly damaged by an earthquake, he set in motion the rebuilding and expansion of the building.

KEY VERSE: Intelligent people are always ready to learn. Their ears are open for knowledge. (Prov. 18:15 NLT)

Hugo (M)

MEANING: "thinker"

SIGNIFICANCE: Hugo Grotius (1583–1645) first forwarded the idea of the oceans being international territory for all nations to use for trade. As the first Christian apologist, his book in defense of the Christian faith, published in 1632, stayed in print in several languages until the end of the nineteenth century.

KEY VERSE: Understanding is a fountain of life to those who have it. (Prov. 16:22)

Husto (SEE JUSTIN)

Hyacinth (F)

MEANING: "purple flower"

SIGNIFICANCE: Saint Hyacinth (1185–1257) (a man) became a friend of Saint Dominic and brought the Dominican Order to his native Poland. He then proceeded to preach

H

throughout Poland, Sweden, Norway, Denmark, Scotland, Russia, Turkey, and Greece.

KEY VERSE: If God cares so wonderfully for wildflowers that are here today and thrown into the fire tomorrow, he will certainly care for you. (Matt. 6:30 NLT)

9

"REMEMBER THAT A MAN'S NAME IS, TO
HIM, THE SWEETEST AND MOST IMPORTANT
SOUND IN ANY LANGUAGE."

— DALE CARNEGIE

𝒪

Ignatius (M)

MEANING: "fiery"

SIGNIFICANCE: Saint Ignatius (died c. 115) was likely a disciple of apostles Peter and John and died in the Roman arena as a martyr. Several of his letters have survived to this day and include the first known naming of the "Lord's day," rather than the Sabbath, as a day of worship.

KEY VERSE: Love flashes like fire, the brightest kind of flame. (Song 8:6 NLT)

Ike (SEE ISAAC)

Ilai (M/F)

MEANING: "light"

SIGNIFICANCE: In the Bible, Ilai was one of David's warriors.

KEY VERSE: The LORD is my light and my salvation—whom shall I fear? The LORD is the stronghold of my life—of whom shall I be afraid? (Ps. 27:1)

Ilan (SEE ALON)

Ilona (SEE HELEN)

Imana (F)

MEANING: "faith"

SIGNIFICANCE: Saint Imana (died 1270) was a Cistercian Benedictine nun and abbess of two different convents.

KEY VERSE: Let your roots grow down into him, and let your lives be built on him. Then your faith will grow strong in the truth you were taught, and you will overflow with thankfulness. (Col. 2:7 NLT)

Imma (F)

MEANING: "whole"

SIGNIFICANCE: Saint Imma (c. 700–752) was an abbess at Karlburg, Franconia.

KEY VERSE: So you'll go out in joy, you'll be led into a whole and complete life. The mountains and hills will lead the parade, bursting with song. All the trees of the forest will join the procession, exuberant with applause. (Isa. 55:12 MSG)

Ina (F)

MEANING: "pure"

SIGNIFICANCE: Saint Ina (died 727), King of Wessex, England, abdicated his throne to make a pilgrimage to Rome, where he lived the rest of his life completing acts of penance as a monk.

KEY VERSE: Even a child is known by his actions, by whether his conduct is pure and right. (Prov. 20:11)

Irais (M/F)

MEANING: "rainbow"

SIGNIFICANCE: Saint Irais (died c. 300) was martyred during the persecutions of Roman emperor Diocletian. Nothing is known of his life.

KEY VERSE: When I see the rainbow in the clouds, I will remember the eternal covenant between God and every living creature on earth. (Gen. 9:16 NLT)

Isaac (M)

MEANING: "laughter"

SIGNIFICANCE: In the Bible, Isaac was the promised son of Abraham born when Abraham was a hundred years old.

J

KEY VERSE: Let the righteous rejoice in the LORD and take refuge in him; let all the upright in heart praise him! (Ps. 64:10)

Isabel (F)

MEANING: "devoted to God"

SIGNIFICANCE: Though Saint Isabel of France (died 1270) was a princess, she was a model of humility and other virtues, and remained solely dedicated to God throughout her life.

KEY VERSE: Protect me, for I am devoted to you. Save me, for I serve you and trust you. You are my God. (Ps. 86:2 NLT)

Isabella (F)

MEANING: "my God is bountiful"

SIGNIFICANCE: Born Isabella Baumfree, Sojourner Truth (1797–1883) was a former slave who traveled the country preaching and speaking on behalf of abolition and women's rights. At different times she met with both Harriet Beecher Stowe and President Abraham Lincoln.

KEY VERSE: I will sing to the LORD, because He has dealt bountifully with me. (Ps. 13:6 NASB)

Isaiah (M)

MEANING: "God is my helper"

SIGNIFICANCE: In the Bible, Isaiah was a prophet, often considered as the greatest of the writing prophets.

KEY VERSE: The Lord is my helper; I will not be afraid. (Heb. 13:6)

Ishmael (M)

MEANING: "God hears"

SIGNIFICANCE: In the Bible, Ishmael was the firstborn son of Abraham and his only son by his servant Hagar.

KEY VERSE: God has surely listened and heard my voice in prayer. (Ps. 66:19)

Israel (M)

MEANING: "God perseveres"

SIGNIFICANCE: In the Bible, God changed Jacob's name to Israel when the two of them wrestled, because, God said, "You have struggled with God and with men and have overcome" (Gen. 32:28).

KEY VERSE: You guide me with your counsel, leading me to a glorious destiny. (Ps. 73:24 NLT)

Ita (F)

MEANING: "thirsty"

SIGNIFICANCE: Saint Ita (died c. 570) founded a convent in County Limerick, Ireland, and also a school for boys in another region. One of her students there was Saint Brendan.

KEY VERSE: The Lamb at the center of the throne will be their shepherd; he will lead them to springs of living water. (Rev. 7:17)

Ivan (M)

MEANING: "glorious gift"

SIGNIFICANCE: Saint Ivan was a ninth-century Bohemian courtier who renounced his high position to become a hermit.

KEY VERSE: Children are a gift from the LORD; they are a reward from him. (Ps. 127:3 NLT)

I

Ivo (M)

MEANING: "yew wood"

SIGNIFICANCE: Saint Ivo of Kermartin (1253–1303) was a lawyer who often defended the poor without charge and ministered to them in prison while they awaited trial. He built a hospital from his own funds, served the poor in it, and gave away food grown on his own land to feed them.

KEY VERSE: You will know at last that I, the LORD, am your Savior and Redeemer.... I will exchange your bronze for gold, your iron for silver, your wood for bronze, and your stones for iron. I will make peace your leader and righteousness your ruler! (Isa. 60:16–17 NLT)

Ivy (F)

MEANING: "vine"

SIGNIFICANCE: The ivy plant is a symbol of love and fidelity.

KEY VERSE: I am the vine; you are the branches. Those who remain in me, and I in them, will produce much fruit. For apart from me you can do nothing. (John 15:5 NLT)

J

"REMEMBER THAT A MAN'S
NAME IS, TO HIM, THE
SWEETEST AND MOST
IMPORTANT SOUND IN ANY
LANGUAGE."

— DALE CARNEGIE

J

Jaalah (M/F)

MEANING: "wild goat"

SIGNIFICANCE: In the Bible, Jaalah was a servant of King Solomon whose descendents returned from the Babylonian captivity.

KEY VERSE: Your righteousness is like the mighty mountains, your justice like the ocean depths. You care for people and animals alike, O LORD. (Ps. 36:6 NLT)

Jaan (SEE CHRISTIAN)

Jabez (M)

MEANING: "sorrow"

SIGNIFICANCE: In the Bible, Jabez was noted for his godliness and his prayer for protection, which God answered.

KEY VERSE: Jabez cried out to the God of Israel, "Oh, that you would bless me and enlarge my territory! Let your hand be with me, and keep me from harm." (1 Chron. 4:10)

Jacob (M)

MEANING: "supplanter"

SIGNIFICANCE: In the Bible, Jacob was the grandson of Abraham and a forefather of the nation of Israel.

KEY VERSE: I'll give you a new heart, put a new spirit in

you. I'll remove the stone heart from your body and replace it with a heart that's God-willed, not self-willed. I'll put my Spirit in you and make it possible for you to do what I tell you and live by my commands. (Ezek. 36:26–27 MSG)

Jackson (M)

MEANING: "God has shown favor"

SIGNIFICANCE: Jackson Kemper (1789–1870) was an Episcopal bishop chosen to be a missionary to the unsettled North American West. Throughout his ministry, he urged a more extensive outreach to Native Americans as well as translations of the Bible into their languages.

KEY VERSE: Surely, O LORD, you bless the righteous; you surround them with your favor as with a shield. (Ps. 5:12)

Jacynth (SEE HYACINTH)

Jadah (M/F)

MEANING: "knowing"

SIGNIFICANCE: In the Bible, Jadah was a descendent of King Saul.

KEY VERSE: Knowing what is right is like deep water in the heart; a wise person draws from the well within. (Prov. 20:5 MSG)

J

Jadon (M/F)

MEANING: "Jehovah has heard"

SIGNIFICANCE: In the Bible, Jadon was one of the men who worked on rebuilding the wall of Jerusalem after the return from the exile.

KEY VERSE: My heart has heard you say, "Come and talk with me." And my heart responds, "LORD, I am coming." (Ps. 27:8 NLT)

Jael (M/F)

MEANING: "ascend"

SIGNIFICANCE: In the Bible, Jael helped her countrymen defeat the Canaanites by killing their general.

KEY VERSE: If I rise on the wings of the dawn, if I settle on the far side of the sea, even there your hand will guide me, your right hand will hold me fast. (Ps. 139:9–10)

Jago (SEE JAMES)

Jahleel (M)

MEANING: "hope in God"

SIGNIFICANCE: In the Bible, Jahleel was a son of Zebulun and grandson of Jacob.

KEY VERSE: May your unfailing love rest upon us, O LORD, even as we put our hope in you. (Ps. 33:22)

Jahmai (M)

MEANING: "warm"

SIGNIFICANCE: In the Bible, Jahmai was a son of Tola from the tribe of Issachar.

KEY VERSE: God wants the combination of his steady, constant calling and warm, person counsel in Scripture to come to characterize us, keeping us alert for whatever he will do next. (Rom. 15:4 MSG)

Jaime (SEE JAMES)

Jair (M)

MEANING: "my light"

SIGNIFICANCE: In the Bible, Jair was one of the judges of Israel.

KEY VERSE: The LORD is my light and my salvation—whom shall I fear? The LORD is the stronghold of my life—of whom shall I be afraid? (Ps. 27:1)

Jakim (M)

MEANING: "confirming"; "establishing"

SIGNIFICANCE: In the Bible, Jakim was the family leader of the twelfth group of Aaron's descendents assigned to temple duty during the rule of King David.

KEY VERSE: Let the favor of the Lord our God be

upon us; and confirm for us the work of our hands; yes, confirm the work of our hands. (Ps. 90:17 NASB)

Jalon (M/F)

MEANING: "tarrying"

SIGNIFICANCE: In the Bible, Jalon was a son of Caleb, one of the two spies Moses sent into the Promised Land who came back assuring the Israelites that God would give them the land.

KEY VERSE: Lead me in Your truth and teach me, for You are the God of my salvation; for You I wait all the day. (Ps. 25:5 NASB)

James (M)

MEANING: "supplanter"

SIGNIFICANCE: In the Bible, James was a half brother of Jesus, a leading elder in the church at Jerusalem, and the author of the book of the Bible that bears his name.

KEY VERSE: I'll give you a new heart, put a new spirit in you. I'll remove the stone heart from your body and replace it with a heart that's God-willed, not self-willed. I'll put my Spirit in you and make it possible for you to do what I tell you and live by my commands. (Ezek. 36:26–27 MSG)

Jamie (SEE JAMES)

J

Jamin (M)

MEANING: "right hand"

SIGNIFICANCE: In the Bible, Jamin was one of the men who taught the law to the people after Ezra read it publicly.

KEY VERSE: Your arm is endued with power; your hand is strong, your right hand exalted. (Ps. 89:13)

Janae (SEE JANE)

Janani (M/F)

MEANING: "heart"; "soul"

SIGNIFICANCE: Janani Luwum (1922–77), archbishop of Uganda (Church of England) during the time of Idi Amin's rule, was arrested on trumped-up charges and killed. Several months later, about 25,000 Ugandans gathered at the capital to celebrate the centennial of the first preaching of the gospel in their country. Among the participants were many who had forsaken Christianity but had returned as a result of their seeing the courage of Archbishop Luwum and his companions as they faced death.

KEY VERSE: Guard my soul and deliver me; do not let me be ashamed, for I take refuge in You. (Ps. 25:20 NASB)

Jane (F)

MEANING: "the Lord is gracious"

SIGNIFICANCE: Jane Austen (1775–1817) was an English novelist whose understanding of and insight into women's lives have made her one of the most noted and influential novelists of that time. Her best-known works include *Sense and Sensibility, Pride and Prejudice,* and *Emma.*

KEY VERSE: The LORD is compassionate and gracious, slow to anger, abounding in love. (Ps. 103:8)

Janelle (SEE JANE)

Jania (SEE JANE)

Jared (M)

MEANING: "descending"

SIGNIFICANCE: In the Bible, Jared was a descendent of Seth (son of Adam and Eve) and the father of Enoch.

KEY VERSE: Cast your cares on the LORD and he will sustain you; he will never let the righteous fall. (Ps. 55:22)

Jarratt (M)

MEANING: "spear strong"

SIGNIFICANCE: Devereux Jarratt (1733–1801) was

an American preacher who emulated John Wesley and initiated a revival in North Carolina and Virginia.

KEY VERSE: Sun and moon stood in their places; they went away at the light of Your arrows, at the radiance of Your gleaming spear. (Hab. 3:11 NASB)

Jasia (SEE JANE)

Jason (M)

MEANING: "healer"

SIGNIFICANCE: The Bible says Paul stayed in Jason's home in Thessalonica. According to legend, he was the bishop of Tarsus in Cilicia.

KEY VERSE: O LORD, if you heal me, I will truly be healed; if you save me, I will truly be saved. (Jer. 17:14 NLT)

Jay (M)

MEANING: "rejoiced in"

SIGNIFICANCE: William Jay (1769–1853) is considered one of the greatest English preachers of the nineteenth century and was also the author of the best-selling devotional *Evening and Morning Exercises.*

KEY VERSE: Rejoice in the LORD, O you righteous! For praise from the upright is beautiful. (Ps. 33:1 NKJV)

J

Jedaiah (M)

MEANING: "hand of the Lord"

SIGNIFICANCE: In the Bible, Jedaiah was a descendent of Aaron and head of the second of the twenty-four priestly divisions for temple service in King David's time.

KEY VERSE: I have set the LORD always before me. Because he is at my right hand, I will not be shaken. (Ps. 16:8)

Jedidiah (M)

MEANING: "loved by God"

SIGNIFICANCE: In the Bible, God told Nathan the prophet to give Solomon, David's second son by Bathsheba, this name shortly after his birth.

KEY VERSE: For you bless the godly, O LORD; you surround them with your shield of love. (Ps. 5:12 NLT)

Jemimah (F)

MEANING: "dove"

SIGNIFICANCE: In the Bible, Jemimah was the first of Job's three daughters born after his affliction.

KEY VERSE: Because you are my help, I will sing in the shadow of your wings. (Ps. 63:7)

Jemma (SEE GEMMA)

Jemmie (SEE JEMIMAH)

Jennice (SEE JANE)

Jerahmeel (M)

MEANING: "mercy of God"

SIGNIFICANCE: In the Bible, Jerahmeel was a Levite family leader who served in the sanctuary during King David's reign.

KEY VERSE: Do not withhold your mercy from me, O LORD; may your love and your truth always protect me. (Ps. 40:11)

Jeremiah (M)

MEANING: "appointed by Jehovah"

SIGNIFICANCE: Jeremiah was a prophet to Judah before its fall in 586 BC. Though his messages were often of judgment and doom, God promised Jeremiah protection and deliverance despite opposition.

KEY VERSE: [God] chose us in [Christ] before the creation of the world to be holy and blameless in his sight. (Eph. 1:4)

Jeremy (M)

MEANING: "exalted of the Lord"

SIGNIFICANCE: Saint Jeremy (died 309), along with four companions, ministered to Christians who were condemned to work the mines of Cilicia during the persecutions of Maximus. His work exposed his faith, which resulted in his execution.

KEY VERSE: The fear of man brings a snare, but he who trusts in the LORD will be exalted. (Prov. 29:25 NASB)

Jeriah (M/F)

MEANING: "taught by Jehovah"

SIGNIFICANCE: In the Bible, Jeriah was one of the Levites David appointed to manage religious and civil affairs in his kingdom.

KEY VERSE: Teach me your way, O LORD, and I will walk in your truth; give me an undivided heart, that I may fear your name. (Ps. 86:11)

Jeriel (M/F)

MEANING: "vision of God"

SIGNIFICANCE: In the Bible, Jeriel was a son of Tola from the tribe of Issachar.

KEY VERSE: I'm sure now I'll see God's goodness in the exuberant earth. Stay with GOD! Take heart. Don't quit. I'll say it again: Stay with GOD. (Ps. 27:13 MSG)

Jerome (M)

MEANING: "holy name"

SIGNIFICANCE: Jerome (345–420) was the first person to translate the Bible into Latin using the original Hebrew and Greek texts. His "Vulgate" translation was used for translation work up until the time of the Reformation. Jerome summed up his appreciation for the Bible this way: "Make knowledge of the Scriptures your love.... Live with them, meditate on them, make them the sole object of your knowledge and inquiries."

KEY VERSE: We're depending on GOD; he's everything we need. What's more, our hearts brim with joy since we've taken for our own his holy name. Love us, GOD, with all you've got—that's what we're depending on. (Ps. 33:20–21 MSG)

Jerona (SEE JEROME)

Jerusha (F)

MEANING: "inheritance"

SIGNIFICANCE: In the Bible, Jerusha was the wife of King Uzziah.

KEY VERSE: You are not your own; you were bought at a price. Therefore honor God with your body. (1 Cor. 6:19–20)

Jesaia (SEE ISAIAH)

Jesse (M/F)

MEANING: "God exists"

SIGNIFICANCE: In the Bible, Jesse was the grandson of Ruth and Boaz and the father of King David.

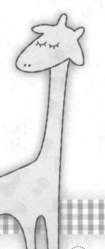

KEY VERSE: The LORD lives! Praise be to my Rock! Exalted be God my Savior! (Ps. 18:46)

Jeva (SEE GENEVIEVE)

Jewel (F)

MEANING: "precious gem"

KEY VERSE: Lips that speak knowledge are a rare jewel. (Prov. 20:15)

Jill (SEE JULIA)

Jilliana (SEE JULIA)

Joah (M)

MEANING: "brother of the Lord"

SIGNIFICANCE: In the Bible, Joah was a recorder under King Josiah and one of the deputies who oversaw the temple repairs.

KEY VERSE: Jesus replied, "My mother and my brothers are all those who hear God's word and obey it." (Luke 8:21 NLT)

Joan (F)

MEANING: "God is gracious"

SIGNIFICANCE: As a teenager, Joan of Arc (1412–31) saw visions and heard voices of Saint Catherine, Saint Margaret, and the archangel

J

Michael encouraging her to save France. She convinced King Charles VII to let her lead troops into battle and, dressed as a man, emerged victorious. Her following conquests were not so successful, however, and she was captured and sold to the English, who convinced church authorities to put her on trial for witchcraft. She was convicted and martyred, but twenty-three years later her sentence was overturned.

KEY VERSE: The LORD is compassionate and gracious, slow to anger, abounding in love. (Ps. 103:8)

Joanna (F)

MEANING: "God is gracious"

SIGNIFICANCE: In the Bible, Joanna was healed by Jesus and helped to support him. She was also among the women who found Jesus' tomb empty after his crucifixion and resurrection.

KEY VERSE: The LORD is compassionate and gracious, slow to anger, abounding in love. (Ps. 103:8)

Joda (M/F)

MEANING: "he shall add"

SIGNIFICANCE: Joda was the son of Joanan and a forefather of Jesus.

KEY VERSE: Wisdom will multiply your days and add years to your life. (Prov. 9:11 NLT)

Jody (SEE JOAN)

Joed (M)

MEANING: "Jehovah is witness"

SIGNIFICANCE: In the Bible, Joed was a descendent of Benjamin and lived in Jerusalem during the time of Nehemiah.

KEY VERSE: The Spirit Himself bears witness with our spirit that we are children of God. (Rom. 8:16 NKJV)

Joel (M)

MEANING: "Jehovah is God"

SIGNIFICANCE: Joel was a prophet who wrote the biblical book bearing his name.

KEY VERSE: How awesome is the LORD Most High, the great King over all the earth. (Ps. 47:2)

Johanan (M)

MEANING: "who is merciful"

SIGNIFICANCE: In the Bible, Johanan was one of David's warriors who was specially trained to handle both shield and spear, to endure hardship, and to move quickly.

J

KEY VERSE: What does the LORD require of you? To act justly and to love mercy and to walk humbly with your God. (Mic. 6:8)

John (M)

MEANING: "grace of God"

SIGNIFICANCE: In the Bible, John the Baptist was a wilderness prophet who preached repentance and was appointed by God to announce the arrival of Jesus

KEY VERSE: For the LORD God is our sun and shield. He gives us grace and glory. The LORD will withhold no good thing from those who do what is right. (Ps. 84:11 NLT)

Joly (F)

MEANING: "happiness" (variant of Jolie)

SIGNIFICANCE: Henri Joly (1839–1925) was a well-respected psychologist and author of *The Psychology of the Saints*. He believed many of the saints shared common characteristics and that those characteristics were not unattainable to the average Christian.

KEY VERSE: Make me walk along the path of your commands, for that is where my happiness is found. (Ps. 119:35 NLT)

Jonah (M)

MEANING: "dove"

SIGNIFICANCE: Jonah the prophet is best known for disobeying God when God told him to preach to the Assyrians in Nineveh. Jonah's choice put him in the belly of a great fish that, upon Jonah's repentance, spat him out onto the shore.

KEY VERSE: Because you are my help, I will sing in the shadow of your wings. (Ps. 63:7)

Jonas (SEE JONAH)

Jonathan (M)

MEANING: "given of God"

SIGNIFICANCE: Jonathan was the son of King Saul, a brave warrior, and David's closest friend.

KEY VERSE: Children are a gift from the LORD; they are a reward from him. (Ps. 127:3 NLT)

Jordan (M)

MEANING: "descending"

SIGNIFICANCE: In the Bible, the Jordan River was the site of many miracles, including the Israelites' crossing with Joshua and the healing of Naaman's leprosy. Also, John the Baptist baptized Jesus there.

KEY VERSE: Cast your cares on the LORD and he will sustain you; he will never let the righteous fall. (Ps. 55:22)

J

Joseph (M)

MEANING: "he shall add"

SIGNIFICANCE: In the Bible, Joseph was a descendent of David and the husband of Mary the mother of Jesus.

KEY VERSE: Wisdom will multiply your days and add years to your life. (Prov. 9:11 NLT)

Joshua (M)

MEANING: "Jehovah saves"

SIGNIFICANCE: In the Bible, Joshua was Moses' assistant and successor. He led the Israelites into the Promised Land and in their battles to conquer it.

KEY VERSE: My shield is God Most High, who saves the upright in heart. (Ps. 7:10)

Josiah (M)

MEANING: "Jehovah supports"

SIGNIFICANCE: Josiah was a king of Judah who sought after God, cleaned out the temple, and revived the practice of obeying God's law.

KEY VERSE: God is the strength of my heart and my portion forever. (Ps. 73:26)

Josko (SEE JOSEPH)

J

Jovita (M/F)

MEANING: "Jupiter"

SIGNIFICANCE: Legendary Saint Jovita (died 120) was a zealous preacher in Milan, Rome, Naples, and elsewhere. He was martyred during the persecutions of Roman emperor Hadrian.

KEY VERSE: Look up into the heavens. Who created all the stars? He brings them out like an army, one after another, calling each by its name. Because of his great power and incomparable strength, not a single one is missing. (Isa. 40:26 NLT)

Jubal (M)

MEANING: "he that runs"

SIGNIFICANCE: In the Bible, Jubal was a descendent of Cain and is credited with being the first musician and inventor of the harp and flute.

KEY VERSE: Keep watch over me and keep me out of trouble; don't let me down when I run to you (Ps. 25:20 MSG)

Jubilee (F)

MEANING: "celebration"

SIGNIFICANCE: God instituted Jubilee—a year of celebration and forgiveness—to occur every fifty years.

KEY VERSE: Shout with joy to God, all the earth! Sing the glory of his name; make his praise glorious! (Ps. 66:1–2)

Jud (M)

MEANING: "praised"

SIGNIFICANCE: Leo Jud (1492–1542) was a Swiss theologian and reformer. He was a colleague of Ulrich Zwingli and participated in the translation of the Zurich Bible.

KEY VERSE: God ... you keep me going when times are tough—my bedrock, GOD, since my childhood. I've hung on you from the day of my birth, the day you took me from the cradle; I'll never run out of praise. (Ps. 71:4–6 MSG)

Judah (M)

MEANING: "praise"

SIGNIFICANCE: Judah was the fourth of Jacob's sons but received the birthright privileges of the firstborn when Jacob blessed his sons. Both the lines of David and Jesus come from the tribe of Judah.

KEY VERSE: God ... you keep me going when times are tough—my bedrock, GOD, since my childhood. I've hung on you from the day of my birth, the day you took me from the cradle; I'll never run out of praise. (Ps. 71:4–6 MSG)

Jude (M)

MEANING: "right in the law"

SIGNIFICANCE: Jude was the brother of James and wrote the biblical book bearing his name.

KEY VERSE: The mouth of the righteous man utters wisdom, and his tongue speaks what is just. (Ps. 37:30)

Judith (F)

MEANING: "praise"

SIGNIFICANCE: Saint Judith (c. 1200–1260) practiced a mystical and contemplative form of Christianity. After her husband died and her children were raised, Judith disposed of her property and spent the rest of her life in contemplation and caring for the sick.

KEY VERSE: God ... you keep me going when times are tough—my bedrock, GOD, since my childhood. I've hung on you from the day of my birth, the day you took me from the cradle; I'll never run out of praise (Ps 71:4–6 MSG)

Judson (M)

MEANING: "Jude's son"

SIGNIFICANCE: When Adoniram Judson (1788–1850) began his forty-year career as a missionary to Burma (now Myanmar) he set a goal of translating the Bible into Burmese and establishing a church of one hundred members before he died. At the time of his death, he left the Bible, one hundred churches, and more than eight thousand Christian believers in Burma.

KEY VERSE: The mouth of the righteous man utters wisdom, and his tongue speaks what is just. (Ps. 37:30)

Julia (F)

MEANING: "youthful"

SIGNIFICANCE: Saint Julia Billiart (1751–1816) took a vow of chastity at age fourteen and committed her life to serving and teaching the poor. She founded the Congregation of the Sisters of Notre Dame, an organization dedicated to the Christian education of girls.

KEY VERSE: You are my hope, O Lord GOD; You are my trust from my youth. (Ps. 71:5 NKJV)

Julian (M)

MEANING: "youthful"

SIGNIFICANCE: Saint Julian (died c. 302) and his wife converted their home into a hospital that housed up to a thousand patients. He was later martyred during the persecutions of Roman emperor Diocletian.

KEY VERSE: You are my hope, O Lord GOD; You are my trust from my youth. (Ps. 71:5 NKJV)

J

Juliana (F)

MEANING: "youthful"

SIGNIFICANCE: The husband of Saint Juliana of Bologna (died 435) left her, with her blessing, to become a priest. Thereafter, she raised her four children alone and then devoted herself to God and service to the poor.

KEY VERSE: You are my hope, O Lord GOD; You are my trust from my youth. (Ps. 71:5 NKJV)

Julina (SEE JULIA)

Julius (M)

MEANING: "downy"

SIGNIFICANCE: Saint Julius the Veteran (255–302) was a Christian and a veteran soldier of the Imperial Roman Army. When Julius was denounced by fellow soldiers, the authorities tried to bribe him into abandoning his faith. Julius declined and was martyred.

KEY VERSE: He will cover you with his feathers. He will shelter you with his wings. His faithful promises are your armor and protection. (Ps. 91:4 NLT)

Justa (F)

MEANING: "fair"

SIGNIFICANCE: Saint Justa was a potter. A wealthy client offered to buy several vessels for a significant sum. When Justa and her sister learned that the pots would be used in pagan rituals, they smashed them all. The girls were later arrested and martyred for their act.

KEY VERSE: Blessed be GOD, my mountain, who trains me to fight fair and well. He's the bedrock on which I stand, the castle in which I live, my rescuing knight, the high crag where I run for dear life. (Ps. 144:1 MSG)

Justina (F)

MEANING: "righteous"

SIGNIFICANCE: Saint Justina was martyred for her faith by the Huns.

KEY VERSE: Surely, O LORD, you bless the righteous; you surround them with your favor as with a shield. (Ps. 5:12)

Justus (M)

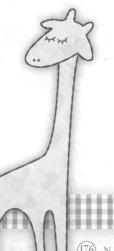

MEANING: "upright"

SIGNIFICANCE: In the Bible, Justus was a Corinthian Christian who opened his home to Paul and other Christians after the Jewish synagogue was closed to Paul's preaching.

KEY VERSE: Consider the blameless, observe the upright; there is a future for the man of peace. (Ps. 37:37)

K

"REMEMBER THAT A MAN'S NAME IS, TO
HIM, THE SWEETEST AND MOST IMPORTANT
SOUND IN ANY LANGUAGE."

— DALE CARNEGIE

K

Kaleb (SEE CALEB)

Karl (M)

MEANING: "manly"

SIGNIFICANCE: Saint Karl Leisner (1915–45) was imprisoned for criticizing Adolf Hitler but was secretly ordained in Dachau concentration camp. He was still there when the camp was liberated, but due to illness, he was transferred to a sanitarium where he spent the remaining months of his life.

KEY VERSE: The LORD is my light and my salvation; whom shall I fear? The LORD is the strength of my life; of whom shall I be afraid? (Ps. 27:1 NKJV)

Kea (M/F)

MEANING: "white"

SIGNIFICANCE: The legends of Saint Kea (seventeenth century) relate his dealings with King Arthur, in which Kea negotiates peace between Arthur and Mordred, and chastises Guinevere for her unfaithfulness to Arthur. Some have identified Saint Kea with Sir Kay of Arthurian legend.

KEY VERSE: All who are victorious will be clothed in white. I will never erase their names from the Book of Life, but I will announce before my Father and his angels that they are mine. (Rev. 3:5 NLT)

Kelvin (M)

MEANING: "from the narrow river"

SIGNIFICANCE: William Thomson (First Baron Kelvin) (1824–1907) was a devout Christian known for developing the Kelvin temperature scale and for his inventions and improvements in the field of electricity.

KEY VERSE: How precious is your unfailing love, O God! All humanity finds shelter in the shadow of your wings. You feed them from the abundance of your own house, letting them drink from your river of delights. (Ps. 36:7–8 NLT)

Ken (M)

MEANING: "strong"

SIGNIFICANCE: Thomas Ken (1637–1711) is best known as the author of the "Doxology," which begins "Praise God from whom all blessings flow."

KEY VERSE: Be strong in the Lord and in his mighty power. (Eph. 6:10)

Kenan (M)

MEANING: "owner"

SIGNIFICANCE: Saint Kenan (died 489) knew Saint Patrick and was admired by him for his writing skills. Building a cathedral on the site of a pagan altar he had destroyed, he was the first in Ireland to use stone to do so.

KEY VERSE: You are not your own; you were bought at a price. Therefore honor God with your body. (1 Cor. 6:19–20)

Kennera (M)

MEANING: "brave chieftain"

SIGNIFICANCE: Saint Kennera was educated with Saint Ursula and later became a nun and recluse.

KEY VERSE: Wait patiently for the LORD. Be brave and courageous. Yes, wait patiently for the LORD. (Ps. 27:14 NLT)

Kenneth (M)

MEANING: "handsome"

SIGNIFICANCE: Saint Kenneth was the son of a chieftain and later became a hermit.

KEY VERSE: You're the handsomest of men; every word from your lips is sheer grace, and God has blessed you. (Ps. 45:2 MSG)

Kennocha (M/F)

MEANING: "lovely"

SIGNIFICANCE: Though born wealthy, Saint Kennocha (died 1007) rejected a materialistic existence, feeling called to a life of prayer.

KEY VERSE: Whatever is true, whatever is noble, whatever is right, whatever is pure, whatever is

lovely, whatever is admirable—if anything is excellent or praiseworthy—
think about such things. (Phil. 4:8)

Kevin (M)

MEANING: "gentle"

SIGNIFICANCE: Saint Kevin (c. 498–618) lived with monks from age
twelve and later founded a monastery. Because he lived as a hermit for
many years of his life, he was noted as a man who preferred the company
of animals to people. One legend relates that as he stood one day during
Lent, his arms outstretched in prayer, a blackbird laid an egg in Kevin's
hand. Kevin stood still until the baby bird hatched.

KEY VERSE: As God's chosen people, holy and dearly loved, clothe yourselves
with compassion, kindness, humility, gentleness and patience. (Col. 3:12)

Keyna (F)

MEANING: "jewel"

SIGNIFICANCE: Saint Keyna was a recluse in Cornwall, England, where a
church bears her name.

KEY VERSE: Lips that speak knowledge are a rare jewel. (Prov. 20:15)

Kezia (M/F)

MEANING: "sweet-scented spice"

SIGNIFICANCE: In the Bible, Kezia was Job's
second daughter born after he became
prosperous once again.

KEY VERSE: Walk in love, as Christ also has loved us and given Himself for us, an offering and a sacrifice to God for a sweet-smelling aroma. (Eph. 5:2 NKJV)

Kiara (F)

MEANING: "dark"

SIGNIFICANCE: Saint Kiara (died 680) was a nun who lived in a place in County Tipperary, Ireland, that is now named Kilkeary in her honor.

KEY VERSE: You light a lamp for me.. The LORD, my God, lights up my darkness. (Ps. 18:28 NLT)

Kieran (M/F)

MEANING: "dark"

SIGNIFICANCE: Saint Kieran (died c. 530) was ordained by Saint Patrick, founded a monastery, and has several healing wells named for him.

KEY VERSE: You light a lamp for me.. The LORD, my God, lights up my darkness. (Ps. 18:28 NLT)

Killian (M/F)

MEANING: "battle"

SIGNIFICANCE: Saint Killian (c. 640–689) was a monk who traveled as a missionary with eleven others through Gaul to Würzburg. Killian's New Testament was preserved in

Würzburg Cathedral until 1803 and now resides in the university library.

KEY VERSE: Praise be to the LORD my Rock, who trains my hands for war, my fingers for battle. (Ps. 144:1)

Kinnia (F)

MEANING: unknown

SIGNIFICANCE: Saint Kinnia (fifth century) was a nun and baptized by Saint Patrick.

KEY VERSE: The LORD leads with unfailing love and faithfulness all who keep his covenant and obey his demnds. (Ps. 25:10 NLT)

Kino (M)

MEANING: "to set in motion"

SIGNIFICANCE: Saint Eusebio Francisco Kino (1645–1711) is remembered for establishing more than twenty missions in northwestern Mexico and the southwestern United States and for his strong opposition to the Spaniards using the Sonoran Indians as forced labor in the silver mines.

KEY VERSE: I have set the LORD always before me; because He is at my right hand I shall not be moved. (Ps. 16:8 NKJV)

Kirk (M)

MEANING: "church"

SIGNIFICANCE: The church is the representation of Christ on earth.

KEY VERSE: Let us aim for harmony in the church and try to build each other up. (Rom. 14:19 NLT)

Kit (SEE CHRISTIAN)

Klaus (SEE NICHOLAS)

Kore (M/F)

MEANING: "pure"

SIGNIFICANCE: In the Bible, Kore was a Levite and porter at the east gate of the temple.

KEY VERSE: Create in me a pure heart, O God, and renew a steadfast spirit within me. (Ps. 51:10)

Kris (SEE CHRISTIAN)

Krista (SEE CHRISTIAN)

Kyle (SEE KENNOCHA)

"REMEMBER THAT A MAN'S NAME IS, TO HIM, THE SWEETEST AND MOST IMPORTANT SOUND IN ANY LANGUAGE."

— DALE CARNEGIE

L

Laeta (F)

MEANING: "happy"

SIGNIFICANCE: Saint Jerome wrote these words in the fourth or fifth century to a woman named Laeta: "I am telling you this, Laeta, devoted daughter of Christ, so that you do not despair and give up hope for your father's salvation."

KEY VERSE: May the righteous be glad and rejoice before God; may they be happy and joyful. (Ps. 68:3)

Lana (SEE HELEN)

Lancelot (M)

MEANING: "servant"

SIGNIFICANCE: Lancelot Andrewes (1555–1626), bishop of Winchester, was part of the committee of scholars that produced the King James Version of the Bible, and he probably contributed more to it than any other single person.

KEY VERSE: Your word is a lamp to my feet and a light for my path. (Ps. 119:105)

Landry (M/F)

MEANING: "ruler"

SIGNIFICANCE: Saint Landry (died c. 661) was the bishop of Paris and founded the first hospital there. He is noted for his work with the poor.

KEY VERSE: May the nations be glad and sing for joy, for you rule the peoples justly and guide the nations of the earth. (Ps. 67:4)

Laura (F)

MEANING: "laurel"

SIGNIFICANCE: Laura Ingalls Wilder (1867–1957) is the author of the beloved Little House series of books, which she did not begin until she was sixty-three years old.

KEY VERSE: May the favor of the Lord our God rest upon us; establish the work of our hands for us—yes, establish the work of our hands. (Ps. 90:17)

Laurel (SEE LAWRENCE)

Laurette (SEE LAURA)

Lawrence (M)

MEANING: "fierce"

SIGNIFICANCE: Saint Lawrence (died 258) kept the church's money from the Roman government by giving it to the poor. When a greedy leader demanded the treasure, Lawrence presented him with the poor and sick, saying, "This is the church's treasure!"

KEY VERSE: GOD makes his people strong. GOD gives his people peace. (Ps. 29:11 MSG)

Leah (F)

MEANING: "weary"

SIGNIFICANCE: In the Bible, Leah was the first wife of Jacob and the older sister of his second wife, Rachel. Though Leah was not Jacob's favorite, she bore him a daughter and six sons, including the two whose tribes became most important in Israel: Levi and Judah.

KEY VERSE: The LORD works righteousness and justice for all the oppressed. (Ps. 103:6)

Leigh (SEE WESLEY)

Lelia (F)

MEANING: "well spoken"

SIGNIFICANCE: Saint Lelia was a princess who became a superior of a convent in Munster. Several Irish place names honor her memory.

KEY VERSE: Well-spoken words bring satisfaction; well-done work has its own reward. (Prov. 12:14 MSG)

Lemuel (M)

MEANING: "dedicated to God"

SIGNIFICANCE: In the Bible, parts of the book of Proverbs are credited to King Lemuel.

KEY VERSE: Commit everything you do to the LORD. Trust him, and he will help you. (Ps. 37:5 NLT)

Leo (M)

MEANING: "lion"

SIGNIFICANCE: Pope Leo I (Leo the Great) (400–461) was the first widely known pope and stopped the invasion of Italy by Attila the Hun using moral persuasion.

KEY VERSE: The righteous are as bold as a lion. (Prov. 28:1)

Leonadra (SEE LEONARDO)

Leonardo (M)

MEANING: "lion"

SIGNIFICANCE: Leonardo da Vinci (1452–1519) is known for his paintings *Mona Lisa* and *The Last Supper.* But he was also an inventor whose conceptualizations of the tank, helicopter, calculator, and solar power were far ahead of their time.

KEY VERSE: The righteous are as bold as a lion. (Prov. 28:1)

Leone (SEE LEO)

Leonista (SEE LEO)

Levi (M)

MEANING: "joined in harmony"

SIGNIFICANCE: In the Bible, Levi was a son of Jacob and the father of the priestly tribe.

KEY VERSE: If we walk in the light, as he is in the light, we have fellowship with one another. (1 John 1:7)

L

Levon (SEE LEVI)

Lewis (M)

MEANING: "famous in war"

SIGNIFICANCE: C. S. Lewis (1898–1963) is the beloved author of more than twenty-five books including the Chronicles of Narnia series, *The Screwtape Letters,* and *Mere Christianity.*

KEY VERSE: Praise be to the LORD my Rock, who trains my hands for war, my fingers for battle. (Ps. 144:1)

Lexi, Lexie (SEE ALEXANDRA)

Liam (SEE WILLIAM)

Lilias (F)

MEANING: "pure"

SIGNIFICANCE: Lilias Trotter (1853–1928) gave up a promising career as an artist to become a missionary to the Sufis of North Africa, a calling that could have easily resulted in her death.

KEY VERSE: Whatever is true, whatever is noble, whatever is right, whatever is pure, whatever is lovely, whatever is admirable—if anything is excellent or praiseworthy—think about such things. (Phil. 4:8)

Lillian (F)

MEANING: "innocence"

L

SIGNIFICANCE: Saint Lillian (died c. 852) initially lived as a secret Christian, unwilling to expose herself to possible persecution. Stories of others boldly living their faith, however, inspired her to do the same. She was later martyred with her husband.

KEY VERSE: The LORD rewarded me for doing right. He has seen my innocence. (Ps. 18:24 NLT)

Lily (F)
MEANING: "lily flower"

SIGNIFICANCE: Saint Lily of Madrid (1565–1624) was a nun noted for her life of penance and intense prayer.

KEY VERSE: Flowers appear on the earth; the season of singing has come, the cooing of doves is heard in our land. (Song 2:12)

Lincoln (M)
MEANING: "lake"

SIGNIFICANCE: Abraham Lincoln (1809–65) was the sixteenth president of the United States, during which time he oversaw the Union war effort during the Civil War and planned for the abolition of slavery and the rebuilding of the country.

KEY VERSE: He makes me lie down in green pastures, he leads me beside quiet waters. (Ps. 23:2)

Lindsey (F)
MEANING: "lake"

SIGNIFICANCE: As both a theologian and the historian of the healing movement of the early twentieth century, Gordon Lindsey (1906–73) wrote 250 books on that subject and others.

KEY VERSE: He makes me lie down in green pastures, he leads me beside quiet waters. (Ps. 23:2)

Linus (M)

MEANING: "net"

SIGNIFICANCE: In the Bible, Linus was a Christian in Rome who sent greeting with Paul to Timothy.

KEY VERSE: My eyes are continually toward the LORD, for He will pluck my feet out of the net. (Ps. 25:15 NASB)

Lisette (SEE ELIZABETH)

Lita (SEE CARMEL)

Lito (SEE CHARLES)

Lloyd (M)

MEANING: "dark"

SIGNIFICANCE: William Lloyd Garrison (1805–79) was an abolitionist, journalist, editor of *The Liberator* (a radical abolitionist newspaper), and one of the founders of the American Anti-Slavery Society.

KEY VERSE: You light a lamp for me. The LORD, my God, lights up my darkness. (Ps. 18:28 NLT)

Lois (F)

MEANING: "holy"

SIGNIFICANCE: In the Bible, Lois was the grandmother of Timothy, an early church leader.

KEY VERSE: [God] chose us in [Christ] before the creation of the world to be holy and blameless in his sight. (Eph. 1:4)

Lola (SEE CHARLOTTE)

Lotan (M)

MEANING: "hidden"

SIGNIFICANCE: In the Bible, Lotan was the son of Seir.

KEY VERSE: I have not kept the good news of your justice hidden in my heart; I have talked about your faithfulness and saving power. I have told everyone in the great assembly of your unfailing love and faithfulness. (Ps. 40:10 NLT)

Lotario (SEE LUTHER)

Louis (M)

MEANING: "famous in war"

SIGNIFICANCE: Saint Louis Bertran (1526–81) was a Dominican from the age of eighteen. He was a friend of Saint Teresa of Avila and helped her reform her order. Louis also served as a missionary to Central and South America.

KEY VERSE: Praise be to the LORD my Rock, who trains my hands for war, my fingers for battle. (Ps. 144:1)

Louisa (SEE LOUIS)

Louise (F)

MEANING: "famous in war"

SIGNIFICANCE: Saint Louise de Marillac (1591–1660) devoted her life to helping Saint Vincent de Paul serve the needs of the poor. She said, "Be diligent in serving the poor. Love the poor, honor them, as you would honor Christ himself."

KEY VERSE: Praise be to the LORD my Rock, who trains my hands for war, my fingers for battle. (Ps. 144:1)

Lucas (SEE LUCIUS)

Lucia (F)

MEANING: "graceful light"

SIGNIFICANCE: Saint Lucia Filippini (1672–1732) trained schoolteachers and even founded a group devoted to the education of young girls. Pope Clement XI called her to Rome to establish a school there.

KEY VERSE: The LORD is my light and my salvation—whom shall I fear? The LORD is the stronghold of my life—of whom shall I be afraid? (Ps. 27:1)

Lucian (M)

MEANING: "light"

SIGNIFICANCE: Saint Lucian (died c. 250) spent his early years as a sorcerer, but became a Christian later in life, devoting his time to studying the faith rather than magic.

KEY VERSE: The LORD is my light and my salvation—whom shall I fear? The LORD is the stronghold of my life—of whom shall I be afraid? (Ps. 27:1)

Luciana (SEE LUCY)

Lucius (M)

MEANING: "bringer of light"

SIGNIFICANCE: In the Bible, Lucius was a man from Cyrene listed in the book of Acts among a list of prophets and teachers in Antioch.

KEY VERSE: You, O LORD, keep my lamp burning; my God turns my darkness into light. (Ps. 18:28)

Lucy (F)

MEANING: "bringer of light"

SIGNIFICANCE: Saint Lucy of Syracuse

L

(c. 283–c. 304) vowed her life to Christ in spite of her mother's arranging a marriage for her. Lucy put off the marriage for three years, during which time she prayed for healing for her mother's long-term illness. God granted her request, and her mother cancelled the marriage.

KEY VERSE: The LORD is my light and my salvation—whom shall I fear? The LORD is the stronghold of my life—of whom shall I be afraid? (Ps. 27:1)

Luke (M)

MEANING: "light giving"

SIGNIFICANCE: In the Bible, Luke was the writer of both the gospel of Luke and the book of Acts, a trained physician, and a faithful and humble companion of the apostle Paul.

KEY VERSE: The LORD is my light and my salvation—whom shall I fear? The LORD is the stronghold of my life—of whom shall I be afraid? (Ps. 27:1)

Luther (M)

MEANING: "famous people"

SIGNIFICANCE: Martin Luther (1483–1546) is considered to be the father of the Protestant Reformation. By nailing his ninety-five theses to the door of the Castle Church, he set in motion sweeping change throughout the church, the effects and benefits of which are experienced to this day.

KEY VERSE: O my people, trust in him at all times. Pour out your heart to him, for God is our refuge. (Ps. 62:8 NLT)

Lydia (F)

MEANING: "standing pool"

SIGNIFICANCE: In the Bible, Lydia was a Gentile who was converted to Christianity through Paul's preaching. She later hosted Paul and Silas in her home.

KEY VERSE: As the deer pants for streams of water, so my soul pants for you, O God. (Ps. 42:1)

$\mathcal{M}$

"REMEMBER THAT A MAN'S NAME IS, TO
HIM, THE SWEETEST AND MOST IMPORTANT
SOUND IN ANY LANGUAGE."

— DALE CARNEGIE

$\mathcal{M}$

Macaliano (SEE MICHAEL)

Macaria (M/F)

MEANING: "happy"

SIGNIFICANCE: Saint Macaria was an African martyr. Nothing is known about his life.

KEY VERSE: May the righteous be glad and rejoice before God; may they be happy and joyful. (Ps. 68:3)

Maccalin (M)

MEANING: "son of a warrior"

SIGNIFICANCE: Saint Maccalin (died 978) was a Benedictine monk and later an abbot of two different monasteries.

KEY VERSE: Praise be to the LORD my Rock, who trains my hands for war, my fingers for battle. (Ps. 144:1)

Macrina (F)

MEANING: "tall"

SIGNIFICANCE: Macrina the Younger (330–379) devoted her life to prayer and charitable work. After her father died, she and her mother founded a community of women who shared Macrina's devotion. She often brought poor women home to be clothed, fed, and cared for, and many joined the community.

KEY VERSE: You know me inside and out, you hold me together, you never fail to stand me tall in your presence so I can look you in the eye. (Ps. 41:11 MSG)

Mada (SEE MADELEINE)

Madalena (SEE MADELEINE)

Madeleine (F)

MEANING: "tower"

SIGNIFICANCE: Saint Madeleine Fontaine (1723–94) and three of her convent sisters were arrested by French revolutionaries and sentenced to death for refusing to take the Oath of the Constitution.

KEY VERSE: The name of the LORD is a strong tower; the righteous run to it and are safe. (Prov. 18:10)

Madelina (SEE MADELEINE)

Madison (M/F)

MEANING: "son of a great soldier"

SIGNIFICANCE: Dorothea "Dolley" Madison (1768–1849), wife of President James Madison, was raised a Quaker and noted as a gracious hostess with a sparkling personality. Her most lasting achievement was her rescue of state papers, a painting of George Washington, and other national treasures before the British Army burned the White House in 1814.

KEY VERSE: How great is the love the Father has lavished on us, that we should be called children of God! And that is what we are! (1 John 3:1)

Madge (SEE MARGARET)

Magnus (M)

MEANING: "great"

SIGNIFICANCE: Several legends surround Saint Magnus of Füssen (died c. 666). In one, as Magnus walked near his monastery, he encountered a bear that showed him a vein of iron ore. When he gave the bear some cake, the bear led him to several other sources of iron in the mountains nearby, thus establishing the area's most profitable industry.

KEY VERSE: How great is the love the Father has lavished on us, that we should be called children of God! And that is what we are! (1 John 3:1)

Mahan (M)

MEANING: "great"

SIGNIFICANCE: Asa Mahan (1799–1889) was the first president of Oberlin College, the first coed college in the world. He was so proud of his position on women's rights that he wanted it engraved on his tombstone!

KEY VERSE: How great is the love the Father has lavished on us, that we should be called children of God! And that is what we are! (1 John 3:1)

Mahlah (F)

MEANING: "pardon"

SIGNIFICANCE: In the Bible, Mahlah was one of five sisters who appealed to Moses to arrange for them to keep their inheritance in the Promised Land in spite of their having no brothers.

KEY VERSE: O Lord, you are so good, so ready to forgive, so full of unfailing love for all who ask for your help. (Ps. 86:5 NLT)

Mahli (M/F)

MEANING: "pardon"

SIGNIFICANCE: In the Bible, Mahli was a grandson of Levi and a founder of the Mahlite family, who were appointed to carry the frames of the Tent of Meeting and the pillars of the court.

KEY VERSE: O Lord, you are so good, so ready to forgive, so full of unfailing love for all who ask for your help. (Ps. 86:5 NLT)

M

Maisie (SEE MARGARET)

Malachi (M)

MEANING: "angel"

SIGNIFICANCE: The prophet Malachi is the author of the book of the Bible that bears his name. Nothing is known of his life.

KEY VERSE: The angel of the LORD encamps around those who fear him, and he delivers them. (Ps. 34:7)

Marana (M/F)

MEANING: "thicket"

SIGNIFICANCE: Saints Marana (fifth century) and Cyra were two hermits who were said to have kept holy silence every day of the year except on Whitsunday (Pentecost).

KEY VERSE: Let the fields and their crops burst out with joy! Let the trees of the forest rustle with praise before the LORD! (Ps. 96:12–13 NLT)

Marcella (F)

MEANING: "warring"

SIGNIFICANCE: Saint Marcella (325–410) organized a group of religious women at her mansion under the spiritual direction of Jerome. When captured by the Goths who invaded Rome, she was tortured to give up her treasure but released when the men realized she had already given everything away to the poor.

KEY VERSE: Praise be to the LORD my Rock, who trains my hands for war, my fingers for battle. (Ps. 144:1)

Marciana (F)

MEANING: "hammer"

$\mathcal{M}$

SIGNIFICANCE: Saint Marciana (died 303) was a young Christian girl who was killed after being accused of vandalizing a statue of the goddess Diana (Artemis).

KEY VERSE: The words of the wise prod us to live well. They're like nails hammered home, holding life together. They are given by God, the one Shepherd. (Eccl. 12:11 MSG)

Marco (M)

MEANING: "warring"

SIGNIFICANCE: Marco Polo (1254–1324) was a Venetian trader and explorer who was one of the first to travel the Silk Road (a series of interconnected trade routes) to China and to visit Kublai Khan (grandson of Genghis Kahn) of Mongol.

KEY VERSE: Praise be to the LORD my Rock, who trains my hands for war, my fingers for battle. (Ps. 144:1)

Marcus (SEE MARK)

Mareas (M)

MEANING: "confused"

SIGNIFICANCE: Saint Mareas (died 360) was a bishop in Persia and martyred in the persecutions of King Sapor II.

KEY VERSE: God is not the author of confusion but of peace. (1 Cor. 14:33 NKJV)

Marelle (SEE MARY)

Marette (SEE MARY)

M

Margaret (F)

MEANING: "pearl"

SIGNIFICANCE: After her conversion to Roman Catholicism, Saint Margaret Clitherow (1556–86) was imprisoned repeatedly for sheltering priests (including a relative) and for permitting secret Masses to be held on her property.

KEY VERSE: You'll be a stunning crown in the palm of GOD's hand, a jeweled gold cup held high in the hand of your God. (Isa. 62:3 MSG)

Margo (SEE MARGARET)

Marguerite (F)

MEANING: "child of light"

SIGNIFICANCE: After her mother died, Saint Marguerite Bourgeous (1620–1700) helped her father raise her eleven siblings. When she was twenty-seven, she received an invitation from the governor of Montreal, Canada, to leave France and teach school in the New World. She said yes and spent the rest of her life in North America.

KEY VERSE: The LORD is my light and my salvation—whom shall I fear? The LORD is the stronghold of my life—of whom shall I be afraid? (Ps. 27:1)

Mari (F)

MEANING: "bitter"

SIGNIFICANCE: Saint Mari (second century) was a zealous missionary who won many converts, destroyed pagan temples, and built churches, monasteries, and convents.

KEY VERSE: May my meditation be sweet to Him; I will be glad in the LORD. (Ps. 104:34 NKJV)

M

Marian (F)

MEANING: "bitter"

SIGNIFICANCE: Maid Marian is the female companion of the legendary Robin Hood. She has been portrayed as both a dainty lady and a skilled archer and adventurer.

KEY VERSE: May my meditation be sweet to Him; I will be glad in the LORD. (Ps. 104:34 NKJV)

Mariel (SEE MARY)

Marinette (F)

MEANING: "of the sea"

SIGNIFICANCE: As a toddler, Saint Marinette (1768–1838) broke her hip and was left unable to walk. Her mother prayed faithfully for years, and one day Marinette was healed. She devoted the remainder of her life to evangelization, care for the poor, and education of both the wealthy and underprivileged.

KEY VERSE: Mightier than the thunder of the great waters, mightier than the breakers of the sea—the LORD on high is mighty. (Ps. 93:4)

Maris (M/F)

MEANING: "of the sea"

SIGNIFICANCE: Upon his conversion, the wealthy Saint Maris (died 270) gave his fortune to the poor. He was later martyred in the persecutions of Roman emperor Aurelian.

KEY VERSE: Mightier than the thunder of the great waters, mightier than the breakers of the sea—the LORD on high is mighty. (Ps. 93:4)

Marita (SEE MARY)

M

Marius (M)

MEANING: "hammer"

SIGNIFICANCE: Saint Marius of Bodon (died 555) founded an abbey and
served as its first abbot.

KEY VERSE: The words of the wise prod us to live well. They're like nails
hammered home, holding life together. They are given by God, the one
Shepherd. (Eccl. 12:11 MSG)

Mark (M)

MEANING: "shining"

SIGNIFICANCE: John Mark was a companion to Barnabas (his cousin),
Paul, and Peter and wrote the biblical book that bears his name.

KEY VERSE: Let your light shine before men, that they may see your good
deeds and praise your Father in heaven. (Matt. 5:16)

Markita (SEE MARCIANA)

Marshall (M)

MEANING: "steward"

SIGNIFICANCE: The Reverend Dr. Peter Marshall (1902–49) was the
minister of the New York Avenue Presbyterian Church in Washington
DC and known for his love and respect for the common person. He
twice served as chaplain to the US Senate.

KEY VERSE: A person who is put in charge as a manager must be faithful.
(1 Cor. 4:2 NLT)

Marta (SEE MARTHA)

Martelle (SEE MARTHA)

M

Martha (F)

MEANING: "lady"

SIGNIFICANCE: In the Bible, Martha was the sister of Mary and Lazarus. When she went out to meet Jesus after Lazarus had died, though she complained to Jesus, she then confessed her belief that he was the Christ.

KEY VERSE: So now you can pick out what's true and fair, find all the good trails! Lady Wisdom will be your close friend, and Brother Knowledge your pleasant companion. Good Sense will scout ahead for danger, Insight will keep an eye out for you. (Prov. 2:9–10 MSG)

Martin (M)

MEANING: "warrior"

SIGNIFICANCE: Martin Luther King Jr. (1929–68) was the most famous leader of the American Civil Rights Movement. His promotion of nonviolence and racial equality earned him the Nobel Peace Prize before his assassination. He is best known for his speech "I Have a Dream."

KEY VERSE: Praise be to the LORD my Rock, who trains my hands for war, my fingers for battle. (Ps. 144:1)

Martina (F)

MEANING: "warring"

SIGNIFICANCE: Saint Martina (died 228) was the daughter of a wealthy Roman Christian. After her parents' deaths, she gave away her inheritance to the poor and devoted herself to prayer. She was later martyred for refusing to sacrifice to pagan gods.

KEY VERSE: Praise be to the LORD my Rock, who trains my hands for war, my fingers for battle. (Ps. 144:1)

_M_

Mary (F)

MEANING: "bitter"

SIGNIFICANCE: Mary was the mother of Jesus the Messiah and the one human being who was with him from his birth to his death.

KEY VERSE: May my meditation be sweet to Him; I will be glad in the LORD. (Ps. 104:34 NKJV)

Marya (SEE MARY)

Maryse (SEE MARY)

Mason (M/F)

MEANING: "worker in stone"

SIGNIFICANCE: John Mason Neale (1818–66) was an Anglican priest and scholar, but he is perhaps best known for the hymns he wrote, such as "All Glory, Laud, and Honor" and "Of the Father's Love Begotten."

KEY VERSE: Because the Sovereign LORD helps me, I will not be disgraced. Therefore, I have set my face like a stone, determined to do his will. And I know that I will not be put to shame. (Isa. 50:7 NLT)

Matanya (M/F)

MEANING: "gift of God"

SIGNIFICANCE: In the Bible, King Zedekiah was also named Matanya.

KEY VERSE: Children are a gift from the LORD; they are a reward from him. (Ps. 127:3 NLT)

Matilda (F)

MEANING: "brave in war"

SIGNIFICANCE: Saint Matilda (c. 895–968) married King Henry I and became queen of Germany. She founded several Benedictine abbeys and was well known throughout her kingdom for giving generously to the poor, teaching the uneducated, comforting the sick, and visiting prisoners.

KEY VERSE: Praise be to the LORD my Rock, who trains my hands for war, my fingers for battle. (Ps. 144:1)

Matthew (M)

MEANING: "gift of God"

SIGNIFICANCE: Matthew was one of the twelve disciples who responded immediately to Jesus' call. In the biblical book that bears his name he makes a point of clarifying for his Jewish audience the ways in which Jesus fulfilled Old Testament prophecies.

KEY VERSE: Children are a gift from the LORD; they are a reward from him. (Ps. 127:3 NLT)

Matthias (M)

MEANING: "gift of God"

SIGNIFICANCE: In the Bible, Matthias was chosen by the apostles as the disciple to take Judas's place.

KEY VERSE: Every good and perfect gift is from above, coming down from the Father of the heavenly lights. (James 1:17)

Maura (F)

MEANING: "wished-for child"

SIGNIFICANCE: The Roman authorities arrested both Saint Maura (died c. 286) and her husband one day, hoping to locate certain sacred texts. Her husband refused to talk, and Maura made a public profession of faith. When the governor ordered her tortured along with her husband, Maura assured onlookers that God was the only protection she needed. Both she and her husband were later martyred.

KEY VERSE: Children are a gift from the LORD; they are a reward from him. (Ps. 127:3 NLT)

Maurice (M)

MEANING: "dark"

SIGNIFICANCE: Saint Maurice (died c. 287) was a Christian officer in charge of a legion of converts in an anti-Christian army. He encouraged his men to stay strong in the faith despite the persecution they faced. When he and his men refused to sacrifice to the gods, they were martyred.

KEY VERSE: You light a lamp for me. The LORD, my God, lights up my darkness. (Ps. 18:28 NLT)

Maximilian (M)

MEANING: "greatest"

SIGNIFICANCE: Saint Maximilian (274–95) was the son of a Roman Army veteran and a conscientious objector. When drafted into the army, he refused to serve, saying that his faith prohibited it. He was martyred for his stand.

KEY VERSE: "Love the Lord your God with all your heart and with all your soul and with all your mind." This is the first and greatest commandment. (Matt 22:37–38)

Maxio (SEE MAXIMILIAN)

Meigan (M/F)

MEANING: "strong and capable"

M

SIGNIFICANCE: Saint Meigan was a Welsh monk.

KEY VERSE: Be strong in the Lord and in his mighty power. (Eph. 6:10)

Mel (M/F)

MEANING: "dark"

SIGNIFICANCE: Saint Mel (died 489) traveled with his uncle, Saint Patrick, evangelizing Ireland. He supported himself by working with his hands and gave to the poor anything beyond what he needed for necessities.

KEY VERSE: You light a lamp for me. The LORD, my God, lights up my darkness. (Ps. 18:28 NLT)

Melaine (M)

MEANING: "dark"

SIGNIFICANCE: Saint Melaine (died 535) was a bishop who was largely responsible for eliminating idol worship in his area.

KEY VERSE: You light a lamp for me. The LORD, my God, lights up my darkness. (Ps. 18:28 NLT)

Melania (F)

MEANING: "dark"

SIGNIFICANCE: Saint Melania (c. 383–439) used her inheritance to support monasteries in Egypt, Syria, and Palestine, and she aided churches and monasteries in Europe. When she made a pilgrimage to the Holy Land with her mother and husband, they settled at Jerusalem. Melania became a friend of Saint Jerome.

KEY VERSE: You light a lamp for me. The LORD, my God, lights up my darkness. (Ps. 18:28 NLT)

M

Melanie (F)

MEANING: "dark"

SIGNIFICANCE: Melanie is the long-suffering wife of Ashley Wilkes in Margaret Mitchell's *Gone with the Wind*.

KEY VERSE: You light a lamp for me. The LORD, my God, lights up my darkness. (Ps. 18:28 NLT)

Melito (M)

MEANING: "to fight"

SIGNIFICANCE: Saint Melito (died c. 180), bishop of Sardis, was the first to list the Christian canon (books) of the Old Testament. He also wrote a famous apology (defense) of Christianity, which he sent to Marcus Aurelius.

KEY VERSE: Blessed be GOD, my mountain, who trains me to fight fair and well. He's the bedrock on which I stand, the castle in which I live, my rescuing knight, the high crag where I run for dear life. (Ps. 144:1 MSG)

Melody (F)

MEANING: "song"

KEY VERSE: Speak to one another with psalms, hymns and spiritual songs. Sing and make music in your heart to the Lord. (Eph. 5:19)

Mendel (M/F)

MEANING: "wisdom"

SIGNIFICANCE: Gregor Mendel (1822–84) is often called the "father of genetics" for his study of the inheritance of traits in pea plants.

KEY VERSE: Fear of the LORD is the foundation of true wisdom. All who obey his commandments will grow in wisdom. Praise him forever! (Ps. 111:10 NLT)

M

Menno (M)

MEANING: "strong"

SIGNIFICANCE: Menno Simons (1496–1561) was a leader of the Dutch Anabaptists (those who rebaptize adults who were baptized as infants) whose followers became known as Mennonites.

KEY VERSE: GOD makes his people strong. GOD gives his people peace. (Ps. 29:11 MSG)

Meraiah (M/F)

MEANING: "resistance"

SIGNIFICANCE: In the Bible, Meraiah was the head of a priestly family in Jerusalem after the return from captivity.

KEY VERSE: Put on every piece of God's armor so you will be able to resist the enemy in the time of evil. Then after the battle you will still be standing firm. (Eph. 6:13 NLT)

Merari (M/F)

MEANING: "strength"

SIGNIFICANCE: In the Bible, Merari was the youngest son of Levi, one of Jacob's sons. Merari's sons were responsible for carrying the frames, bars, pillars, bases, vessels, and accessories of the Tent of Meeting.

KEY VERSE: The LORD will guide you always; he will satisfy your needs in a sun-scorched land and will strengthen your frame. You will be like a well-watered garden, like a spring whose waters never fail. (Isa. 58:11)

Mercy (F)

MEANING: "compassion"

KEY VERSE: What does the LORD require of you? To act justly and to love mercy and to walk humbly with your God. (Mic. 6:8)

Merry (F)

MEANING: "cheerful"

KEY VERSE: May the righteous be glad and rejoice before God; may they be happy and joyful. (Ps. 68:3)

Merryn (M/F)

MEANING: "joyful"

SIGNIFICANCE: Saint Merryn (died c. 620) founded an abbey in Scotland and served as its first abbot.

KEY VERSE: The LORD is my strength and shield. I trust him with all my heart. He helps me, and my heart is filled with joy. I burst out in songs of thanksgiving. (Ps. 28:7 NLT)

Mesha (M/F)

MEANING: "salvation"

SIGNIFICANCE: In the Bible, Mesha was a son of Caleb, the Israelite leader who brought back a favorable report on the Promised Land.

KEY VERSE: My victory and honor come from God alone. He is my refuge, a rock where no enemy can reach me. (Ps. 62:7 NLT)

Micah (M)

MEANING: "who is like the Lord"

SIGNIFICANCE: Micah was a prophet and the author of the biblical book that bears his name.

KEY VERSE: Your righteousness reaches to the skies, O God, you who have done great things. Who, O God, is like you? (Ps. 71:19)

Michael (M)

MEANING: "who is like the Lord"

M

SIGNIFICANCE: In the Bible, Michael is referred to as the "archangel."

KEY VERSE: Your righteousness reaches to the skies, O God, you who have done great things. Who, O God, is like you? (Ps. 71:19)

Michal (F)

MEANING: "who is like the Lord"

SIGNIFICANCE: In the Bible, Michal was a daughter of King Saul and a wife of King David. Though she was punished for rebuking David for dancing in the streets, she also risked her own life to save David's shortly after they were married.

KEY VERSE: Your righteousness reaches to the skies, O God, you who have done great things. Who, O God, is like you? (Ps. 71:19)

Michelina (F)

MEANING: "who is like the Lord"

SIGNIFICANCE: Saint Michelina of Pesaro (1300–1356) was widowed at age twenty and decided to become a nun. Her family opposed her so strongly that they locked her up and declared her insane. When she was finally released, she gave away her wealth and dedicated her life to God's service.

KEY VERSE: Your righteousness reaches to the skies, O God, you who have done great things. Who, O God, is like you? (Ps. 71:19)

Mickella (SEE MICHAEL)

Mikael (M)

MEANING: "who is like the Lord"

SIGNIFICANCE: Mikael Agricola (c. 1510–57), bishop of Turku, saw the importance of his people being able to worship in Finnish and wrote a

M

prayer book, translations of the New Testament, liturgy, and several hymns. He is considered the father of written Finnish.

KEY VERSE: Your righteousness reaches to the skies, O God, you who have done great things. Who, O God, is like you? (Ps. 71:19)

Milari (SEE HILARY)

Miriam (F)

MEANING: "bitter"

SIGNIFICANCE: In the Bible, Miriam was a prophetess and sister of Aaron and Moses.

KEY VERSE: May my meditation be sweet to Him; I will be glad in the LORD. (Ps. 104:34 NKJV)

Mirin (M/F)

MEANING: "bitter"

SIGNIFICANCE: Saint Mirin (died c. 620) evangelized an area of Scotland, founded an abbey, and served as its first abbot.

KEY VERSE: May my meditation be sweet to Him; I will be glad in the LORD. (Ps. 104:34 NKJV)

Mitchell (SEE MICHAEL)

Mitzi (SEE MIRIAM)

Molly (SEE MARY)

Monica (F)

MEANING: "advisor"

SIGNIFICANCE: Saint Monica (322–87) prayed faithfully for her son's conversion. We know him today as Saint Augustine of Hippo.

M

KEY VERSE: The LORD says, "I will guide you along the best pathway for your life. I will advise you and watch over you." (Ps. 32:8 NLT)

Moriah (M/F)

MEANING: "God is my teacher"

SIGNIFICANCE: In the Bible, Mount Moriah was the site of Solomon's temple and is now the site of the Islamic Dome of the Rock.

KEY VERSE: Show me your ways, O LORD, teach me your paths; guide me in your truth and teach me, for you are God my Savior. (Ps. 25:4–5)

Moses (M)

MEANING: "saved"

SIGNIFICANCE: In the Bible, Moses was God's appointed leader who brought the Israelites out of slavery in Egypt to the border of the Promised Land.

KEY VERSE: My victory and honor come from God alone. He is my refuge, a rock where no enemy can reach me. (Ps. 62:7 NLT)

Moss (SEE MOSES)

Mura (M/F)

MEANING: "bitter"

SIGNIFICANCE: Saint Mura (550–c. 645), an abbot appointed by Saint Columba, wrote a rhymed biography of Columba.

KEY VERSE: May my meditation be sweet to Him; I will be glad in the LORD. (Ps. 104:34 NKJV)

Mychal (SEE MICHAEL)

Myles (M)

M

MEANING: "merciful"

SIGNIFICANCE: Myles Coverdale (1488–1568) produced the first complete printed translation of the Bible into English.

KEY VERSE: What does the LORD require of you? To act justly and to love mercy and to walk humbly with your God. (Mic. 6:8)

N

"REMEMBER THAT A MAN'S NAME IS, TO HIM, THE SWEETEST AND MOST IMPORTANT SOUND IN ANY LANGUAGE."

— DALE CARNEGIE

Nahum (M)

MEANING: "comforter"

SIGNIFICANCE: Nahum was a prophet to Israel and wrote the biblical book that bears his name. Nothing else is known about his life.

KEY VERSE: May your unfailing love be my comfort, according to your promise to your servant. (Ps. 119:76)

Nan (SEE HANNAH)

Naomi (F)

MEANING: "pleasant"

SIGNIFICANCE: Naomi was the mother-in-law of Ruth, who is listed in the genealogy of Jesus. Her story is told in the biblical book of Ruth.

KEY VERSE: Pleasant words are a honeycomb, sweet to the soul and healing to the bones. (Prov. 16:24)

Nat (SEE NATHAN)

Natalia (F)

MEANING: "birthday"

SIGNIFICANCE: Though Saint Natalia (died 852) and her husband knew that openly practicing their faith was inviting persecution, they made provision for their children's welfare and began caring for the sick and poor and openly talking about Jesus. Both were martyred.

KEY VERSE: Yes, you have been with me from birth; from my mother's womb you have cared for me. No wonder I am always praising you! (Ps. 71:6 NLT)

Natalina (SEE NATALIA)

Nathan (M)

MEANING: "gift of God"

SIGNIFICANCE: In the Bible, Nathan was a prophet of God and adviser to King David. He fearlessly confronted David regarding his sin with Bathsheba and also played a vital role in developing the musical aspects of temple worship.

KEY VERSE: Every good and perfect gift is from above, coming down from the Father of the heavenly lights. (James 1:17)

Nathanael (M)

MEANING: "gift of God"

SIGNIFICANCE: Jesus called Nathanael to be his disciple and said about him, "Here is a true Israelite, in whom there is nothing false" (John 1:47).

KEY VERSE: Children are a gift from the LORD; they are a reward from him. (Ps. 127:3 NLT)

Neale (M)

MEANING: "champion"

SIGNIFICANCE: John Mason Neale (1818–66) was an Anglican priest and scholar, but he is perhaps best known for the hymns he wrote, such as "All Glory, Laud, and Honor" and "Of the Father's Love Begotten."

KEY VERSE: GOD's now at my side and I'm not afraid; who would dare lay a hand on me? GOD's my strong champion. (Ps. 118:5 MSG)

Nehemiah (M)

MEANING: "comforted by God"

SIGNIFICANCE: In the Bible, Nehemiah was a cupbearer to King Artaxerxes but pled to be allowed to return to Jerusalem to help rebuild the city. Once there, Nehemiah completed the wall and also served as governor, leading his people to religious reform and spiritual awakening.

KEY VERSE: I remember your ancient laws, O LORD, and I find comfort in them. (Ps. 119:52)

Nelliana (SEE HELEN)

Nelo (SEE DANIEL)

Nera (F)

MEANING: "black"

SIGNIFICANCE: Saint Nera (1230–87) was known for her care of the sick.

n

Niccolo (SEE NICHOLAS)

Nicholas (M)

MEANING: "victory of the people"

SIGNIFICANCE: Though many legends surround Saint Nicholas of Myra (fourth century), including Santa Claus and Sinterklaas, all that is known for certain is that he had a reputation for secretly bestowing gifts.

KEY VERSE: Everyone runs; one wins. Run to win. (1 Cor. 9:24 MSG)

Nico (SEE ANTHONY)

Niels (M)

MEANING: "son of the champion"

SIGNIFICANCE: Niels Seno (1638–86) is considered to be the founder of geology.

KEY VERSE: GOD's now at my side and I'm not afraid; who would dare lay a hand on me? GOD's my strong champion. (Ps. 118:5 MSG)

Nixie (SEE BERNICE)

N

Noadiah (M)

MEANING: "witness of the Lord"

SIGNIFICANCE: In the Bible, Noadiah was one of the two Levites present for the weighing and measuring of the temple treasure that had been brought back to Jerusalem by Ezra.

KEY VERSE: How beautiful on the mountains are the feet of those who bring good news, who proclaim peace, who bring good tidings. (Isa. 52:7)

Noah (M)

MEANING: "rest"

SIGNIFICANCE: Noah is remembered as a righteous man who obeyed God by building an ark in which he and his family, along with a host of animals in pairs, were saved from the flood.

KEY VERSE: Ask where the good way is, and walk in it, and you will find rest for your souls. (Jer. 6:16)

Noel (M)

MEANING: "Christmas"

SIGNIFICANCE: Saint Noel Chabanel (1613–49) was a missionary priest who had difficulty adapting to the languages and customs of the Native Americans, so he decided to proceed on faith and vowed to, if necessary, spend the rest of his life at his work. The Iroquois and Hurons later killed him and other North American martyrs in a violent raid. Soon after the massacre, many Iroquois converted.

KEY VERSE: Everyone who confesses openly his faith in Jesus Christ—the Son of God, who came as an actual flesh-and-blood person—comes from God and belongs to God. (1 John 4:2 MSG)

Noelle (SEE NOEL)

O

"REMEMBER THAT A MAN'S NAME IS, TO HIM, THE SWEETEST AND MOST IMPORTANT SOUND IN ANY LANGUAGE."

— DALE CARNEGIE

O

Obadiah (M)

MEANING: "servant of God"

SIGNIFICANCE: Obadiah was a prophet in Israel and authored the book that bears his name.

KEY VERSE: If anyone serves, he should do it with the strength God provides. (1 Peter 4:11)

Odilia (F)

MEANING: "little wealthy one"

SIGNIFICANCE: Born blind, Saint Odilia (c. 660–720) was given by her parents to a peasant family. Taken in by a convent at age twelve, she gained her sight during her baptism. Odilia joined the abbey and eventually became its abbess.

KEY VERSE: Humility and the fear of the LORD bring wealth and honor and life. (Prov. 22:4)

Oleksa (M)

MEANING: "holy"

SIGNIFICANCE: Saint Oleksa Zarytsky (1912–63) was a Greek Catholic pastor imprisoned for his faith and sentenced to ten years in a forced labor camp in the Ukraine. Released for only a short while, he was again arrested for the same reason and spent three more years in prison, where he died.

O

KEY VERSE: [God] chose us in [Christ] before the creation of the world to be holy and blameless in his sight. (Eph. 1:4)

Olena (SEE HELEN)

Oliva, Olive (SEE OLIVIA)

Oliver (M)

MEANING: "peaceful"

SIGNIFICANCE: Saint Oliver Plunkett (1629–81) was an archbishop of Ireland during anti-Catholic persecutions. Though he had to go into hiding, he was determined to continue shepherding his people. Later, he chose to die rather than give false evidence against other bishops.

KEY VERSE: The LORD gives strength to his people; the LORD blesses his people with peace. (Ps. 29:11)

Olivia (F)

MEANING: "peaceful"

SIGNIFICANCE: According to legend, Saint Olivia was captured and deported. Her captors observed her miracles and strong faith, and, wanting to get rid of her, abandoned her in the forest. Some hunters found her, and she brought them to faith. Finally, authorities had her killed, and at the moment of her death, her soul was seen flying to heaven in the form of a dove.

KEY VERSE: The LORD gives strength to his people; the LORD blesses his people with peace. (Ps. 29:11)

Omada (SEE AIMEE)

Omar (M)

MEANING: "eloquent"

SIGNIFICANCE: In the Bible, Omar was a grandson of Esau and the great-grandson of Abraham.

KEY VERSE: If we love each other, God lives in us, and his love is brought to full expression in us. (1 John 4:12 NLT)

Ophrah (M)

MEANING: "fawn"

SIGNIFICANCE: In the Bible, Ophrah was a member of the tribe of Judah.

KEY VERSE: He makes my feet like the feet of a deer; he enables me to stand on the heights. (Ps. 18:33)

Oren (M)

MEANING: "pine tree"

SIGNIFICANCE: In the Bible, Oren was a son of Jerahmeel.

KEY VERSE: [Wisdom] is a tree of life to those

who embrace her; those who lay hold of her will be blessed. (Prov. 3:18)

Otto (M)

MEANING: "wealthy"

SIGNIFICANCE: Saint Otto (died 1220), along with several others, was sent by Francis of Assisi to evangelize in Italy, Seville, and Morocco, where he was martyred.

KEY VERSE: Humility and the fear of the LORD bring wealth and honor and life. (Prov. 22:4)

Ovid (M/F)

MEANING: "worker"

SIGNIFICANCE: Roman poet Ovid (43 BC–AD 17) wrote on love, abandoned women, and mythological transformations, and his work influenced European literature and art for centuries after his death.

KEY VERSE: Whatever you do, work at it with all your heart, as working for the Lord, not for men. (Col. 3:23)

Owen (M)

MEANING: "young warrior"

SIGNIFICANCE: Owen Feltham (c. 1602–68) is known for his book of witty, original, and some have even said brilliant, essays titled *Resolves, Divine, Moral, and Political.*

O

KEY VERSE: Praise be to the LORD my Rock, who trains my hands for war, my fingers for battle. (Ps. 144:1)

Ozman (M)

MEANING: "divine"

SIGNIFICANCE: Agnes Ozman (1870–1937) is considered to be the first in the modern era to have spoken in tongues, thus sparking the Pentecostal-Holiness movement of the early twentieth century.

KEY VERSE: By his divine power, God has given us everything we need for living a godly life. We have received all of this by coming to know him, the one who called us to himself by means of his marvelous glory and excellence. (2 Peter 1:3 NLT)

E

"REMEMBER THAT A MAN'S NAME IS, TO HIM, THE SWEETEST AND MOST IMPORTANT SOUND IN ANY LANGUAGE."

— DALE CARNEGIE

Paavo (SEE PAUL)

Palladia (F)

MEANING: "safeguard"

SIGNIFICANCE: Saint Palladia (second century) was one of a group of wives of martyred soldiers. Following the death of the soldiers, the wives and children were martyred as well.

KEY VERSE: Guard me as as you would guard your own eyes. Hide me in the shadow of your wings. (Ps. 17:8 NLT)

Parnell (SEE PETER)

Pascal (M)

MEANING: "Easter"

SIGNIFICANCE: Blaise Pascal (1623–62) was a French mathematician, physicist, and Christian philosopher. "Pascal's Wager" is a challenge to believe in God. "If you gain, you gain all; if you lose, you lose nothing. Wager, then, without hesitation that He is."

KEY VERSE: It is Christ who died, and furthermore is also risen, who is even at the right hand of God, who also makes intercession for us. (Rom. 8:34 NKJV)

Patience (F)

MEANING: "steadfast expectation"

KEY VERSE: Be still before the LORD and wait patiently for him. (Ps. 37:7)

Patrice (SEE PATRICK)

Patricia (F)

MEANING: "noble"

SIGNIFICANCE: Saint Patricia of Nicomedia (died 304) and her whole family were martyred together.

KEY VERSE: The noble man makes noble plans, and by noble deeds he stands. (Isa. 32:8)

Patrick (M)

MEANING: "noble"

SIGNIFICANCE: Over the course of thirty-three years, Saint Patrick (c. 390–c. 464) effectively converted Ireland. In the Middle Ages Ireland became known as the "land of saints," and during the Dark Ages its monasteries were the great repositories of learning in Europe, all a consequence of Patrick's ministry.

KEY VERSE: The noble man makes noble plans, and by noble deeds he stands. (Isa. 32:8)

Paul (M)

MEANING: "little"

SIGNIFICANCE: The apostle Paul was transformed by God from being a persecutor of early Christians to a preacher who traveled throughout the Roman Empire spreading the good news of God's love.

KEY VERSE: The one who knows much says little; an understanding person remains calm. (Prov. 17:27 MSG)

Paula (F)

MEANING: "little"

SIGNIFICANCE: When Saint Paula (347–404) was widowed, she devoted the rest of her life to spiritual development and care for the poor.

KEY VERSE: The one who knows much says little; an understanding person remains calm. (Prov. 17:27 MSG)

Pawley (SEE PAUL)

Paxton (SEE PATRICK)

Payla (SEE PAUL)

Peace (F)

MEANING: "tranquility"

KEY VERSE: The LORD gives strength to his people; the LORD blesses his people with peace. (Ps. 29:11)

Pearl (F)

MEANING: "lustrous gem"

KEY VERSE: We, who with unveiled faces all

reflect the Lord's glory, are being transformed into his likeness. (2 Cor. 3:18)

Penelope (F)

MEANING: "weaver"

SIGNIFICANCE: In Homer's *Odyssey*, Penelope was married to Odysseus. When her husband was presumed dead by others, she held off suitors by promising to marry when she finished weaving a tapestry. To keep from completing her project, she unraveled each day's work at night. Odysseus finally returned after twenty years.

KEY VERSE: I want you woven into a tapestry of love, in touch with everything there is to know of God. Then you will have minds confident and at rest, focused on Christ. (Col. 2:2 MSG)

Penny (SEE PENELOPE)

Perez (M)

MEANING: "divided"

SIGNIFICANCE: In the Bible, Perez was a son of Judah and thus an ancestor of David and Jesus.

KEY VERSE: I am convinced that nothing can ever separate us from God's love. Neither death nor life, neither angels nor demons, neither our fears for today nor our worries for tomorrow—not even the powers of hell can separate us from God's love. (Rom. 8:38 NLT)

P

Periquin (SEE PETER)

Perla (SEE PEARL)

Perri (SEE PEARL)

Perrin (SEE PETER)

Peter (M)

MEANING: "stone"

SIGNIFICANCE: The apostle Peter was a leader among the disciples and also one of the three within the inner circle. Though he denied Christ just prior to the crucifixion, his sermon on the day of Pentecost resulted in more than five thousand people coming to faith.

KEY VERSE: The LORD has become my fortress, and my God the rock in whom I take refuge. (Ps. 94:22)

Peyton (SEE PATRICK)

Phelisiana (SEE FELICE)

Philip (M)

MEANING: "lover of horses"

SIGNIFICANCE: In the Bible, Philip became an evangelist and was one of the first to obey Christ's command to take the gospel to all people.

KEY VERSE: Some trust in chariots and some in horses, but we trust in the name of the LORD our God. (Ps. 20:7)

Phoebe (F)

MEANING: "shining"

SIGNIFICANCE: In the Bible, Paul commended Phoebe because of her useful service to other Christians.

KEY VERSE: Let your light shine before men, that they may see your good deeds and praise your Father in heaven. (Matt. 5:16)

Pia (F)

MEANING: "pious"

SIGNIFICANCE: Saint Pia was a second-century martyr. No information about her life has survived.

KEY VERSE: Fear of the LORD is the foundation of true wisdom. All who obey his commandments will grow in wisdom. Praise him forever! (Ps. 111:10 NLT)

Piat (M)

MEANING: "goodness"

SIGNIFICANCE: Saint Piat (died c. 286) was an early evangelist to what is now France. He was martyred in the persecutions of Roman emperor Maximian.

KEY VERSE: [God] crowns you with love and

238 NAMES TO LIVE BY

mercy—a paradise crown. He wraps you in goodness—beauty eternal. (Ps. 103:4–5 MSG)

Pico (SEE PETER)

Pier (SEE PETER)

Pip (SEE PHILIP)

Polly (SEE MARY OR PAULA)

Potter (M)

MEANING: "one who shapes clay"

KEY VERSE: O LORD, you are our Father. We are the clay, you are the potter; we are all the work of your hand. (Isa. 64:8)

Priscilla (F)

MEANING: "ancient"

SIGNIFICANCE: In the Bible, Priscilla and her husband, Aquila, were Paul's loyal friends and trusted coworkers. The three of them made tents to support themselves.

KEY VERSE: [God] chose us in [Christ] before the creation of the world to be holy and blameless in his sight. (Eph. 1:4)

Prudence (F)

MEANING: "foresight"; "discretion"

SIGNIFICANCE: A "virtue" name, "Prudence" was popular with the Puritans.

KEY VERSE: Discretion will guard you, understanding will watch over you. (Prov. 2:11 NASB)

Q

"REMEMBER THAT A MAN'S NAME IS, TO HIM, THE SWEETEST AND MOST IMPORTANT SOUND IN ANY LANGUAGE."

— DALE CARNEGIE

Q

Qvenna (SEE QUENTIN)

Qventin (M)

MEANING: "fifth"

SIGNIFICANCE: Saint Quentin (died 287) was the son of a Roman
senator, and his preaching won many to Christ. He was later arrested
during the persecutions of Emperor Maximian.

KEY VERSE: As for me, it is good to be near God. I have made the
Sovereign LORD my refuge; I will tell of all your deeds. (Ps. 73:28)

Qvintana (SEE QUENTIN)

Qviqvi (SEE HENRY)

R

"REMEMBER THAT A MAN'S NAME IS, TO HIM, THE SWEETEST AND MOST IMPORTANT SOUND IN ANY LANGUAGE."

— DALE CARNEGIE

R

Race (M/F)

MEANING: "competition"

KEY VERSE: Everyone runs; one wins. Run to win. (1 Cor. 9:24 MSG)

Rachel (F)

MEANING: "lamb"

SIGNIFICANCE: In the Bible, Rachel was Jacob's favorite wife and gave birth to Joseph and Benjamin.

KEY VERSE: The LORD is my shepherd; I have all that I need. (Ps. 23:1 NLT)

Rafqa (F)

MEANING: "good company"

SIGNIFICANCE: Saint Rafqa (1832–1914) was a nun who prayed one night that she might share in Christ's suffering. Her health soon deteriorated, but she spent as much time as she could in prayer and working in the convent, usually spinning wool and knitting.

KEY VERSE: So now you can pick out what's true and fair, find all the good trails! Lady Wisdom will be your close friend, and Brother Knowledge your pleasant companion. Good Sense will scout ahead for danger, Insight will keep an eye out for you. (Prov. 2:9–10 MSG)

R

Ram (M)

MEANING: "elevated"

SIGNIFICANCE: In the Bible, Ram was an ancestor of King David and is
listed in Matthew's genealogy of Jesus.

KEY VERSE: You are a shield around me, O LORD; you bestow glory on
me and lift up my head. (Ps. 3:3)

Ranieri (M/F)

MEANING: "strong counselor"

SIGNIFICANCE: Saint Ranieri (1117–61) spent his youth as a wild,
partying minstrel. One evening he met a man who shared the gospel
with him. Ranieri had a conversion experience, burned his fiddle, and
became a merchant. His business became quite successful, but Ranieri
felt convicted about his great wealth. He gave it away and became a poor
and penitent monk.

KEY VERSE: GOD makes his people strong. GOD gives
his people peace. (Ps. 29:11 MSG)

Raven (F)

MEANING: "shiny and black"

SIGNIFICANCE: In the Bible, ravens brought food to
the prophet Elijah during a time of famine.

KEY VERSE: Consider the ravens: They do not sow
or reap, they have no storeroom or barn; yet God

feeds them. And how much more valuable you are than birds! (Luke 12:24)

Rebekah (F)

MEANING: "captivating"

SIGNIFICANCE: In the Bible, Rebekah was the wife of Isaac and the mother of Esau and Jacob.

KEY VERSE: Guard Clear Thinking and Common Sense with your life; don't for a minute lose sight of them. They'll keep your soul alive and well, they'll keep you fit and attractive. (Prov. 3:21 MSG)

Ree (SEE REBEKAH)

Reeba (SEE REBEKAH)

Reece (SEE REES)

Reena (SEE CATHERINE)

Rees (M/F)

MEANING: "ardent"

SIGNIFICANCE: Seth Cook Rees (1854–1933), founder of the Pilgrim Holiness Church, was one of the first to embrace the right of women to preach. He demonstrated his belief by inviting his wife to serve alongside him as copastor and coevangelist.

KEY VERSE: Work with enthusiasm, as though you were working for the Lord rather than for people. (Eph. 6:7 NLT)

Regina (F)

MEANING: "queen"

SIGNIFICANCE: Saint Regina (died c. 286) was driven from her home because of her faith and lived as a poor, prayerful shepherdess.

KEY VERSE: You are a chosen people, a royal priesthood, a holy nation, a people belonging to God, that you may declare the praises of him who called you out of darkness into his wonderful light. (1 Peter 2:9)

Reico (SEE RICHARD)

René (M/F)

MEANING: "reborn"

SIGNIFICANCE: Saint Rene Groupil (1606–42) studied medicine and worked as a medic for Jesuit missionaries ministering to the Huron tribe in North America. He was captured and later martyred by the Iroquois, enemies of the Huron.

KEY VERSE: All praise to God, the Father of our Lord Jesus Christ. It is by his great mercy that we have been born again. (1 Peter 1:3 NLT)

Renée (SEE RENE)

R

Renzo (SEE LAWRENCE)

Rephael (M)

MEANING: "God heals"

SIGNIFICANCE: In the Bible, Rephael was a temple gatekeeper in David's time.

KEY VERSE: Your light will break forth like the dawn, and your healing will quickly appear; then your righteousness will go before you, and the glory of the LORD will be your rear guard. (Isa. 58:8)

Reuben (M)

MEANING: "behold a son"

SIGNIFICANCE: Reuben was the eldest son of Jacob and saved his brother Joseph's life by convincing his other brothers to spare Joseph's life.

KEY VERSE: A slave has no permanent place in the family, but a son belongs to it forever. (John 8:35)

Rheba (SEE REBEKAH)

Rhoda (F)

MEANING: "roses"

SIGNIFICANCE: In the Bible, Rhoda was the young woman who answered Peter's knock at the door of the house in which Christians were praying for his release from prison.

R

KEY VERSE: The LORD will guide you always; he will satisfy your needs in a sun-scorched land and will strengthen your frame. You will be like a well-watered garden, like a spring whose waters never fail. (Isa. 58:11)

Rhodia (SEE ROSE)

Richard (M)

MEANING: "strong ruler"

SIGNIFICANCE: Richard Niebuhr (1894–1962) was an American Christian ethicist best known for his book *Christ and Culture* and was most concerned with how humans relate to God, to each other, to their communities, and to the world.

KEY VERSE: GOD makes his people strong. GOD gives his people peace. (Ps. 29:11 MSG)

Risa (SEE ERIC)

Risto (SEE CHRISTIAN)

Rita (SEE MARGARET)

Riva (SEE REBEKAH)

Robert (M)

MEANING: "famous"

SIGNIFICANCE: Robert Hunt (c. 1568–1608) served as chaplain of the expedition that founded

Jamestown. He led the group in morning and evening prayers and preached two sermons each Sunday. He holds the honor of being the first Anglican pastor to reside permanently in North America.

KEY VERSE: LORD, I have heard of your fame; I stand in awe of your deeds, O LORD. Renew them in our day, in our time make them known. (Hab. 3:2)

Robin (M/F)

MEANING: "bright fame"

SIGNIFICANCE: Robin Hood is a legendary outlaw folk hero known in modern tales as one who fought injustice and tyranny and took from the rich to give to the poor.

KEY VERSE: You, O LORD, will sit on your throne forever. Your fame will endure to every generation. (Ps. 102:12 NLT)

Rocco (M)

MEANING: "rock"

SIGNIFICANCE: Saint Rocco Gonzalez (1576–1628) was a Paraguayan noble who worked with the Jesuits to teach indigenous Indians to care for cattle and sheep; and also served as doctor, engineer, architect, farmer, and pastor; and supervised the construction of churches, schools, and homes. Rocco was known for his courage, kindness, and commitment to preserving the culture and customs of the people he served.

KEY VERSE: My victory and honor come from God alone. He is my refuge, a rock where no enemy can reach me. (Ps. 62:7 NLT)

Rock (M)

MEANING: "rock"

KEY VERSE: My victory and honor come from God alone. He is my refuge, a rock where no enemy can reach me. (Ps. 62:7 NLT)

Roderick (M)

MEANING: "famous ruler"

SIGNIFICANCE: Saint Roderick (died 857) was beaten into a coma by his two brothers. One was so angry with him that he announced to authorities that Roderick had converted to Islam. When Roderick awoke, he was questioned about it, and denied the allegation, claiming allegiance to Christ. The authorities took this to be apostasy, deciding Roderick was denying his new Moslem faith. He was imprisoned for several months, and then martyred with another Christian.

KEY VERSE: May the nations be glad and sing for joy, for you rule the peoples justly and guide the nations of the earth. (Ps. 67:4)

Roger (M)

MEANING: "famous spearman"

SIGNIFICANCE: Roger Williams (c. 1603–83) founded Providence in what is now Rhode Island as a result of being driven out of the Plymouth colony. He was a firm advocate of the need for separation between church and state and for freedom of conscience in worship.

KEY VERSE: Sun and moon stood in their places; they went away at the light of Your arrows, at the radiance of Your gleaming spear. (Hab. 3:11 NASB)

Rohelio (SEE ROGER)

Ronan (M/F)

MEANING: "oath"

SIGNIFICANCE: Saint Ronan was a bishop in Ireland and confessor of the faith.

KEY VERSE: I have taken an oath and confirmed it, that I will follow your righteous laws. (Ps. 119:106)

Rory (SEE RODERICK)

Rosa (F)

MEANING: "rose"

SIGNIFICANCE: Rosa Parks (1913–2005) is known for her refusal to obey a bus driver's demand to give

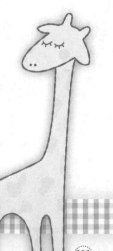

up her seat to a white passenger. Her subsequent arrest and trial was instrumental in launching Martin Luther King Jr. to the forefront of the American Civil Rights Movement. The US Congress dubbed Parks the "Mother of the Modern-Day Civil Rights Movement."

KEY VERSE: If God cares so wonderfully for wildflowers that are here today and thrown into the fire tomorrow, he will certainly care for you. (Matt. 6:30 NLT)

Rosalia (F)

MEANING: "rose"

SIGNIFICANCE: Saint Rosalia (c. 1130–c. 1160) was raised around the Sicilian royal court but knew from a young age that she would dedicate her life to God. As an adult, she moved to a cave and lived the rest of her life there, praying and doing works of penance.

KEY VERSE: The LORD will guide you always; he will satisfy your needs in a sun-scorched land and will strengthen your frame. You will be like a well-watered garden, like a spring whose waters never fail. (Isa. 58:11)

Rosalina (F)

MEANING: "rose"

SIGNIFICANCE: As a child, Saint Rosalina of Villeneuve (1267–1329) was noted for her kindness to the poor, often secretly giving food to beggars outside the family castle. Her father found out and forbade her to continue. She obeyed for a short time but couldn't bear the sight of the beggars outside. According to legend, late one night, she filled her apron with food and started toward the doors. Her father caught her and demanded to know what she carried. When she opened the apron, it was filled with roses. He immediately ordered the cooks to feed everyone at the door.

KEY VERSE: The LORD will guide you always; he will satisfy your needs in a sun-scorched land and will strengthen your frame. You will be like a well-watered garden, like a spring whose waters never fail. (Isa. 58:11)

Rose (F)

MEANING: "rose"

SIGNIFICANCE: Saint Rose of Viterbo (1234–52) was known to preach in the streets from the age of ten. Though she was repeatedly refused entrance to the Poor Clares, upon her death the pope ordered her body laid to rest in the convent.

KEY VERSE: If God cares so wonderfully for wildflowers that are here today and thrown into the fire tomorrow, he will certainly care for you. (Matt. 6:30 NLT)

Ruby (F)

MEANING: "precious red stone"

R

KEY VERSE: [Wisdom] is more precious than rubies; nothing you desire can compare with her. (Prov. 3:15)

Ruellin (M)

MEANING: "famous wolf"

SIGNIFICANCE: Saint Ruellin (died sixth century) was the bishop of Treguier, Brittany, France.

KEY VERSE: The wild animals honor me, the jackals and the owls, because I provide water in the desert and streams in the wasteland, to give drink to my people, my chosen. (Isa. 43:20)

Rufio (SEE RUFUS)

Rufus (M)

MEANING: "red"

SIGNIFICANCE: In the Bible, Rufus was a son of Simon of Cyrene, the man who carried Jesus' cross to Golgotha.

KEY VERSE: God's Word is better than a diamond, better than a diamond set between emeralds. You'll like it better than strawberries in spring, better than red, ripe strawberries. (Ps. 19:10 MSG)

Ruth (F)

MEANING: "friend of beauty"

SIGNIFICANCE: Ruth was a widow and the daughter-in-law of Naomi. Her marriage to Boaz secured her future and Naomi's and established her in the genealogy of David and Jesus.

KEY VERSE: Your beauty should not come from outward adornment.... Instead it should be that of your inner self, the unfading beauty of a gentle and quiet spirit, which is of great worth in God's sight. (1 Peter 3:3–4)

Ruyen (SEE REUBEN)

$\mathcal{S}$

"REMEMBER THAT A MAN'S NAME IS, TO HIM, THE SWEETEST AND MOST IMPORTANT SOUND IN ANY LANGUAGE."

— DALE CARNEGIE

Saccha (SEE SARAH)

Sadella (SEE SARAH)

Salaidh (SEE SARAH)

Saloma (SEE SALOME)

Salome (M/F)

MEANING: "peace"

SIGNIFICANCE: In the Bible, Salome was a follower of Jesus and possibly the sister of Mary (Jesus' mother) and the mother of James and John.

KEY VERSE: Peacemakers who sow in peace raise a harvest of righteousness. (James 3:18)

Samson (M)

MEANING: "like the sun"

SIGNIFICANCE: In the Bible, Samson was a judge known for his great physical strength. Though he failed God many times, God used him to loosen the grip of Philistine oppression of the Israelites.

KEY VERSE: The LORD God is a sun and shield; the LORD bestows favor and honor; no good thing does he withhold from those whose walk is blameless. (Ps. 84:11)

S

Samuel (M)

MEANING: "his name is God"

SIGNIFICANCE: Samuel was a judge and prophet in Israel and anointed both Saul and David as kings.

KEY VERSE: Know that the LORD has set apart the godly for himself; the LORD will hear when I call to him. (Ps. 4:3)

Sandi, Sandie (SEE ALEXANDRA)

Sarah (F)

MEANING: "dawn"

SIGNIFICANCE: Sarah was the wife of Abraham, the cofounder with him of the nation of Israel, and an ancestor of Jesus.

KEY VERSE: Your light will break forth like the dawn, and your healing will quickly appear; then your righteousness will go before you, and the glory of the LORD will be your rear guard. (Isa. 58:8)

Sarette (SEE SARAH)

Saul (M)

MEANING: "asked for"

SIGNIFICANCE: Saul was the first king appointed by God over Israel and was known for his generosity and courage.

KEY VERSE: O Lord, you are so good, so ready

to forgive, so full of unfailing love for all who ask for your help. (Ps. 86:5 NLT)

Sava (M/F)

MEANING: "old"

SIGNIFICANCE: Though born a prince of Serbia, Saint Sava (1176–1235) became a monk, founded several monasteries, and began the reformation and education of his country. Later he translated religious works into Serbian.

KEY VERSE: Remember, O LORD, your great mercy and love, for they are from of old. (Ps. 25:6)

Savina (F)

MEANING: "of the Sabines"

SIGNIFICANCE: Saint Savina of Milan (died 311) was martyred for ministering to prisoners and burying martyrs during the persecutions of Roman emperor Diocletian.

KEY VERSE: He who is kind to the poor lends to the LORD, and he will reward him for what he has done. (Prov. 19:17)

Scarlett (F)

MEANING: "deep red"

SIGNIFICANCE: Scarlett O'Hara is the headstrong and determined heroine of Margaret Mitchell's *Gone with the Wind*.

S

KEY VERSE: God's Word is better than a diamond, better than a diamond set between emeralds. You'll like it better than strawberries in spring, better than red, ripe strawberries. (Ps. 19:10 MSG)

Sean (SEE JOHN)

Sebastian (F)

MEANING: "revered"

SIGNIFICANCE: Johann Sebastian Bach (1685–1750) was the greatest musician and composer of the baroque era. Of his one thousand compositions, nearly three-fourths are intended to be used for worship. He wrote, "At a reverent performance of music, God is always at hand with his gracious presence."

KEY VERSE: Fear of the LORD is the foundation of true wisdom. All who obey his commandments will grow in wisdom. (Ps. 111:10 NLT)

Serah (F)

MEANING: "song"

SIGNIFICANCE: In the Bible, Serah was a daughter of Asher, son of Jacob.

KEY VERSE: The LORD is my strength and shield. I trust him with all my heart. He helps me, and my heart is filled with joy. I burst out in songs of thanksgiving. (Ps. 28:7 NLT)

S

Seraphina (F)

MEANING: "fiery-winged"

SIGNIFICANCE: Saint Seraphina (died 1253) was born to a poor family but found ways to help those who were more destitute than she.

KEY VERSE: Because you are my help, I sing in the shadow of your wings. (Ps. 63:7)

Sergius (M)

MEANING: "net"

SIGNIFICANCE: Saint Sergius (1314–92) was a Russian monk who founded a monastery and contributed to spiritual renewal in his country.

KEY VERSE: My eyes are continually toward the LORD, for He will pluck my feet out of the net. (Ps. 25:15 NASB)

Serra (F)

MEANING: "mountain"

SIGNIFICANCE: Saint Junipero Serra (1713–84) was largely responsible for the establishing and spreading of the Roman Catholic Church on the West Coast of the United States. He founded twenty-one missions, converted thousands of Native Americans, and trained many in European agricultural methods.

KEY VERSE: Blessed be GOD, my mountain, who trains me to fight fair and well. He's the bedrock on which I stand, the castle in which I live, my rescuing knight, the high crag where I run for dear life. (Ps. 144:1 MSG)

Seth (M)

MEANING: "appointed"

SIGNIFICANCE: Seth was the third son of Adam and Eve.

KEY VERSE: How much better to get wisdom than gold, to choose understanding rather than silver! (Prov. 16:16)

Seymour (M)

MEANING: "tailor"

SIGNIFICANCE: William J. Seymour (1870–1922) was an African American minister whose preaching resulted in the Azusa Street Revival, which began the current charismatic and Pentecostal movements.

KEY VERSE: Take my yoke upon you. Let me teach you, because I am humble and gentle at heart, and you will find rest for your souls. For my yoke is easy to bear, and the burden I give you is light. (Matt 11:29–30 NLT)

Shan (SEE JOHN)
Shanna (F)

MEANING: "lily"

SIGNIFICANCE: Lilies are symbols of renewal and resurrection.

KEY VERSE: Consider how the lilies grow. They do not labor or spin. Yet I tell you, not even Solomon in all his splendor was dressed like one of these. (Luke 12:27)

Shara (SEE SHARON)

Sheba (F)

MEANING: "promise"

SIGNIFICANCE: In the Bible, Sheba was a descendent of Noah.

KEY VERSE: The LORD is faithful to all his promises and loving toward all he has made. (Ps. 145:13)

Sheena (SEE JANE)

Sheerah (F)

MEANING: "relationship"

SIGNIFICANCE: In the Bible, Sheerah was a daughter or granddaughter of Ephraim. Her offspring built two towns.

KEY VERSE: The person who lives in right relationship with God does it by embracing what God arranges for him. (Gal. 3:11 MSG)

Shelah (F)

MEANING: "request"

SIGNIFICANCE: In the Bible, Shelah is listed in Luke's genealogy of Jesus.

KEY VERSE: O Lord, you are so good, so ready to forgive, so full of unfailing love for all who ask for your help. (Ps. 86:5 NLT)

Shelina (SEE CELESTE)

Shelley (SEE RACHEL)

Shem (SEE SAMUEL)

Shepherd (M)

MEANING: "caretaker of sheep"

KEY VERSE: The Lamb at the center of the throne will be their shepherd; he will lead them to springs of living water. (Rev. 7:17)

Shifra (F)

MEANING: "beautiful"

SIGNIFICANCE: In the Bible, Shifra (Shiphrah) was one of the midwives who disobeyed the Egyptian pharaoh's order to kill all Israelite babies.

KEY VERSE: Let the beauty of the LORD our God be upon us, and establish the work of our hands for us. (Ps. 90:17 NKJV)

Shiloh (M)

MEANING: "abundance"

SIGNIFICANCE: In the Bible, Shiloh was the place the Tent of Meeting was set up and left until the Philistines took the ark of the covenant.

S

KEY VERSE: How precious is your unfailing love, O God! All humanity finds shelter in the shadow of your wings. You feed them from the abundance of your own house, letting them drink from your river of delights. (Ps. 36:7–8 NLT)

Shua (F)

MEANING: "saving"

SIGNIFICANCE: In the Bible, Shua was Judah's mother-in-law.

KEY VERSE: I know that the LORD saves His anointed; He will answer him from His holy heaven with the saving strength of His right hand. (Ps. 20:6 NKJV)

Shubal (M)

MEANING: "seat of God"

SIGNIFICANCE: Shubal Stearns (1706–71), a Baptist preacher, helped to spread the revival of the Great Awakening throughout Virginia and North Carolina.

KEY VERSE: God reigns over the nations; God is seated on his holy throne. (Ps. 47:8)

Silas (M)

MEANING: "of the forest"

SIGNIFICANCE: Silas, a respected church

leader, was imprisoned with Paul in Philippi, where an earthquake shook open the jail doors, freeing them both.

KEY VERSE: Let the fields and their crops burst out with joy! Let the trees of the forest rustle with praise before the LORD! (Ps. 96:12–13 NLT)

Silverio (M)

MEANING: "of the forest"

SIGNIFICANCE: Pope Silverio (480–537), a humble man, was caught in the middle of a political plot, kidnapped, convicted of a trumped-up charge, and exiled.

KEY VERSE: Let the fields and their crops burst out with joy! Let the trees of the forest rustle with praise before the LORD! (Ps. 96:12–13 NLT)

Silvia (F)

MEANING: "of the forest"

SIGNIFICANCE: Saint Silvia (c. 515–92) was the mother of Pope Gregory the Great. She was known for her piety and the excellent education she provided for both her sons.

KEY VERSE: Let the fields and their crops burst out with joy! Let the trees of the forest rustle with praise before the LORD! (Ps. 96:12–13 NLT)

Simeon (M)

MEANING: "obedient"

SIGNIFICANCE: Simeon, a godly Jew living in Jerusalem, was promised he would live to see the Messiah. The Holy Spirit directed him to the temple, where he met Joseph and Mary and prophesied about Jesus' life.

KEY VERSE: Fear of the LORD is the foundation of true wisdom. All who obey his commandments will grow in wisdom. (Ps. 111:10 NLT)

Simon (M)

MEANING: "he who hears"

SIGNIFICANCE: Simon of Cyrene was forced by the Romans to carry Jesus' cross.

KEY VERSE: Know that the LORD has set apart the godly for himself; the LORD will hear when I call to him. (Ps. 4:3)

Simona (SEE SIMON)

Simone (SEE SIMON)

Sisile (SEE CECILIA)

Sofie (SEE SOPHIA)

Sola (M/F)

MEANING: "alone"

SIGNIFICANCE: Martin Luther put forth four great "solas" of Christianity: *sola scriptura* (by

Scripture alone), *sola Christus* (by Christ alone), *sola gratia* (by grace alone), and *sola fide* (by faith alone).

KEY VERSE: Let your unfailing love surround us, LORD, for our hope is in you alone. (Ps. 33:22 NLT)

Solange (F)

MEANING: "dignified"

SIGNIFICANCE: Saint Solange (died 880) was a young shepherdess who took a vow of chastity, devoting herself to God alone.

KEY VERSE: Treat everyone you meet with dignity. Love your spiritual family. Revere God. (1 Peter 2:14 MSG)

Solina (F)

MEANING: "sunlight"

SIGNIFICANCE: Saint Solina (died c. 290) was martyred for refusing to marry a pagan.

KEY VERSE: The LORD God is a sun and shield; the LORD bestows favor and honor; no good thing does he withhold from those whose walk is blameless. (Ps. 84:11)

Solomon (M)

MEANING: "peace"

SIGNIFICANCE: Solomon, the wisest man who ever lived, was David's son and followed him as king. He built the temple in Jerusalem and

S

wrote the biblical books of Ecclesiastes and Song of Songs, many proverbs, and a few psalms.

KEY VERSE: Peacemakers who sow in peace raise a harvest of righteousness. (James 3:18)

Somona (SEE SIMON)

Sondra (SEE ALEXANDRA)

Sonia (SEE SOPHIA)

Sophia (F)

MEANING: "wisdom"

SIGNIFICANCE: Saint Sophia (second century) is thought to be a personification of the wisdom of God rather than an actual person.

KEY VERSE: Wisdom is supreme; therefore get wisdom. Though it cost all you have, get understanding. (Prov. 4:7)

Sophronia (SEE SOPHIA)

Søren (M)

MEANING: "thunder"

SIGNIFICANCE: Danish philosopher Søren Kierkegaard (1813–55) was the philosopher and theologian who first coined the term "leap of faith" in reference to the choice a person makes to believe in God.

KEY VERSE: Mightier than the thunder of the great waters, mightier than the breakers of the sea—the LORD on high is mighty. (Ps. 93:4)

Soshannah (SEE SUSANNAH)

Sparrow (F)
MEANING: "songbird"

KEY VERSE: Let all who take refuge in you be glad; let them ever sing for joy. Spread your protection over them, that those who love your name may rejoice in you. (Ps. 5:11)

Spring (F)
MEANING: "a source of water"

KEY VERSE: The Lamb at the center of the throne will be their shepherd; he will lead them to springs of living water. (Rev. 7:17)

Stephen (M)
MEANING: "crowned"

SIGNIFICANCE: Stephen was an early church leader known for his faith, wisdom, and grace. He was a gifted teacher and leader and was the first to give his life for the gospel.

KEY VERSE: He crowns you with love and mercy—a paradise crown. He wraps you in goodness—beauty eternal. (Ps. 103:4–5 MSG)

Stone (M)

MEANING: "rock"

KEY VERSE: Because the Sovereign LORD helps me, I will not be disgraced. Therefore, I have set my face like a stone, determined to do his will. And I know that I will not be put to shame. (Isa. 50:7 NLT)

Suleima (SEE SALOME)

Susanna (F)

MEANING: "lily"

SIGNIFICANCE: Susanna was one of the women who ministered to Jesus out of her own resources.

KEY VERSE: Consider how the lilies grow. They do not labor or spin. Yet I tell you, not even Solomon in all his splendor was dressed like one of these. (Luke 12:27)

Susannah (F)

MEANING: "lily"

SIGNIFICANCE: Susannah Wesley (1669–1742), mother of Charles and John (as well as six others who survived infancy), prayed for her children daily and saw to it that they were organized in their personal spiritual development, their academic pursuits, and their theology.

KEY VERSE: Consider how the lilies grow. They do not labor or spin. Yet I tell you, not even Solomon in all his splendor was dressed like one of these. (Luke 12:27)

Sylvester (M)

MEANING: "trees"

SIGNIFICANCE: Pope Sylvester II (c. 950–1003) was the first French pope and a prolific scholar who developed a hydraulic organ that surpassed all previous instruments, in which the air had to be pumped manually to produce sound.

KEY VERSE: [Wisdom] is a tree of life to those who embrace her; those who lay hold of her will be blessed. (Prov. 3:18)

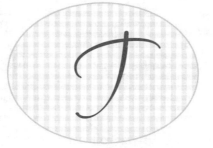

T

"REMEMBER THAT A MAN'S NAME IS, TO
HIM, THE SWEETEST AND MOST IMPORTANT
SOUND IN ANY LANGUAGE."

— DALE CARNEGIE

T

Taavetti (SEE DAVID)

Tabias (M)

MEANING: "talented"

SIGNIFICANCE: Saint Tabias (third or fourth century) was among a group of martyrs at Smyrmium. Nothing is known of his life.

KEY VERSE: May all the gifts and benefits that come from God our Father, and the Master, Jesus Christ, be yours. (1 Cor. 1:3 MSG)

Tabitha (F)

MEANING: "gazelle"

SIGNIFICANCE: In the Bible, Tabitha (also called Dorcas) was a Christian woman noted for her charitable acts. When she died, Peter prayed over her body, and she was raised to life.

KEY VERSE: I run in the path of your commands, for you have set my heart free. (Ps. 119:32)

Tad (SEE THADDEUS)

Tadeo (SEE THADDEUS)

Tahan (M/F)

MEANING: "merciful"

SIGNIFICANCE: In the Bible, Tahan was a son of Ephraim, the younger son of Joseph.

𝒯

KEY VERSE: What does the LORD require of you? To act justly and to love mercy and to walk humbly with your God. (Mic. 6:8)

Talida (F)

MEANING: "sturdy"; "stalwart"

SIGNIFICANCE: Saint Talida of Antinoë (fourth century), head over a group of convents in Egypt, lived more than eighty years as a nun.

KEY VERSE: Keep your eyes open, hold tight to your convictions, give it all you've got, be resolute, and love without stopping. (1 Cor. 16:13 MSG)

Talitha (F)

MEANING: "little girl"

SIGNIFICANCE: When Jesus raised Jairus's twelve-year-old daughter from the dead, he said to her, "'*Talitha koum!* (which means, 'Little girl, I say to you, get up!')" (Mark 5:41).

KEY VERSE: Jesus ... said to them, "Let the little children come to me, and do not hinder them, for the kingdom of God belongs to such as these." (Mark 10:14)

Tam (SEE THOMAS)

Tamar (F)

MEANING: "palm tree"

SIGNIFICANCE: Tamar was a wife of Judah, son of Jacob, and the mother of twins.

T

KEY VERSE: The righteous will flourish like a palm tree ... planted in the house of the LORD, they will flourish in the courts of our God. (Ps. 92:12–13)

Tamara (SEE TAMAR)

Tandy (SEE ANDREW)

Tarea (M/F)

MEANING: "howling"

SIGNIFICANCE: In the Bible, Tarea (also spelled Tahreah) was a descendent of King Saul.

KEY VERSE: The righteous cry out, and the LORD hears them; he delivers them from all their troubles. (Ps. 34:17)

Tathai (M/F)

MEANING: "he has"

SIGNIFICANCE: Saint Tathai (sixth century) founded a monastery school in Wales and was noted for his gentleness, love of country, and generosity to travelers and the poor.

KEY VERSE: Come and see what our God has done, what awesome miracles he performs for his people! (Ps. 66:5 NLT)

Tathan (SEE ATHAN)

Tavis (SEE THOMAS)

Tavor (M/F)

> MEANING: "encampment" (from Tabor)
>
> SIGNIFICANCE: Mount Tabor was the starting point of the battle between the troops of Barak (of Israel) and Sisera (of Canaan) recounted in the book of Judges. The judge Deborah served as Barak's adviser.
>
> KEY VERSE: The angel of the LORD encamps around those who fear him, and he delivers them. (Ps. 34:7)

Taylor (M/F)

> MEANING: "tailor"
>
> SIGNIFICANCE: Hudson Taylor (1832–1905) was a missionary to China known for his zeal for the gospel and the then-radical idea of wearing Chinese clothing and hairstyle. The mission he founded in 1865 continues to operate today.
>
> KEY VERSE: "Has not my hand made all these things, and so they came into being?" declares the LORD. "This is the one I esteem: he who is humble and contrite in spirit, and trembles at my word." (Isa. 66:2)

Te (SEE CLEMENT)

Ted (SEE EDWARD)

Teilo (M)

> MEANING: "hill"

SIGNIFICANCE: Several legends surround Saint Teilo (born c. 500), a Welsh bishop. One says that he tamed a dragon and kept it tied to a rock in the sea to prevent it from harassing a nearby village.

KEY VERSE: So you'll go out in joy, you'll be led into a whole and complete life. The mountains and hills will lead the parade, bursting with song. All the trees of the forest will join the procession, exuberant with applause. (Isa. 55:12 MSG)

Telly (SEE TERENCE)

Temperance (F)
MEANING: "self-control"

KEY VERSE: Better to be patient than powerful; Better to have self-control than to conquer a city. (Prov. 16:32 NLT)

Tempest (F)
MEANING: "storm"

KEY VERSE: The LORD is slow to anger and great in power.... His way is in the whirlwind and the storm. (Nah. 1:3)

Tente (SEE CLEMENT)

Terah (M/F)
MEANING: "breathe"

_T_

SIGNIFICANCE: In the Bible, Terah was the father of Abraham through whom the nation of Israel was born.

KEY VERSE: I will sing to the LORD as long as I live. I will praise my God to my last breath! (Ps. 104:33 NLT)

Terence (M)

MEANING: "tender"

SIGNIFICANCE: Saint Terence was a first-century commander of an imperial Roman bodyguard who witnessed the death sentencing of the apostles John and Paul. He later converted to Christianity and was martyred.

KEY VERSE: Do not withhold Your tender mercies from me, O LORD; let Your lovingkindness and Your truth continually preserve me. (Ps. 40:11 NKJV)

Teresa (F)

MEANING: "reap"

SIGNIFICANCE: Saint Teresa of Avila (1515–82) was a Spanish mystic, monastic reformer, and writer. She wrote, "Let nothing disturb thee; let nothing dismay thee, All things pass; God never changes."

KEY VERSE: So let's not get tired of doing what is good. At just the right time we will reap a harvest of blessing if we don't give up. (Gal. 6:9 NLT)

Teressa (SEE TERESA)

T

Terra (SEE THEODORE)

Terrel (SEE TERENCE)

Tess, Tessa (SEE TERESA)

Thad (SEE THADDEUS)

Thaddeus (M)
MEANING: "courageous"
SIGNIFICANCE: In the Bible, Thaddeus was one of Jesus' twelve disciples.
KEY VERSE: Be strong and let your heart take courage, all you who hope in the LORD. (Ps. 31:24 NASB)

Thea (F)
MEANING: "godly"
SIGNIFICANCE: Saint Thea (died 307) was a dedicated believer who was martyred for her faith.
KEY VERSE: Know that the LORD has set apart the godly for himself; the LORD will hear when I call to him. (Ps. 4:3)

Theodore (M/F)
MEANING: "God-given"
SIGNIFICANCE: Saint Theodore (1798–1856), a French nun, was sent with five other sisters to Vincennes, Indiana, where they founded Saint

Mary-of-the-Woods, the first Catholic women's liberal arts college in the United States.

KEY VERSE: Walk in love, as Christ also has loved us and given Himself for us, an offering and a sacrifice to God for a sweet-smelling aroma. (Eph. 5:2 NKJV)

Thomas (M)

MEANING: "twin"

SIGNIFICANCE: Thomas, one of Jesus' twelve disciples, is best known for his insistence on needing to see and touch Jesus before he would believe in the resurrection. Jesus' appearance to him and his confession of faith ("My Lord and my God") mark the high point of John's gospel.

KEY VERSE: Jesus said to him, "Thomas, because you have seen Me, you have believed. Blessed are those who have not seen and yet have believed." (John 20:29 NKJV)

Tibbie (SEE ISABEL)

Ticha (SEE BEATRICE)

Ticho (SEE PATRICK)

Tiedra (SEE THEODORE)

Tiennot (SEE STEPHEN)

Tieodoro (SEE THEODORE)

Tierney (M/F)

MEANING: "regal"

SIGNIFICANCE: Saint Tierney (died 549) was a monk, and later bishop, known for his intense love of God and his exemplary work ethic.

KEY VERSE: GOD made the heavens—royal splendor radiates from him, a powerful beauty sets him apart. (Ps. 96:5 MSG)

Tillo (M)

MEANING: "rich"

SIGNIFICANCE: Saint Tillo of Solignac (died 702) was kidnapped and sold as a slave. Ransomed by a fellow believer, Tillo became a Benedictine monk, priest, and later missionary in France.

KEY VERSE: Humility and the fear of the LORD bring wealth and honor and life. (Prov. 22:4)

Timiro (SEE TIMOTHY)

Timon (M)

MEANING: "God-fearing"

SIGNIFICANCE: In the Bible, Timon was one of the seven deacons chosen by the apostles to help meet the material needs of the church in Jerusalem.

KEY VERSE: As a father has compassion on his children, so the LORD has compassion on those who fear him. (Ps. 103:13)

𝒯

Timothy (M)

MEANING: "honors God"

SIGNIFICANCE: Timothy was a young believer who traveled with Paul on several occasions. He was highly esteemed by many and known for his loyalty to Paul.

KEY VERSE: You are not your own; you were bought at a price. Therefore honor God with your body. (1 Cor. 6:19–20)

Tiria (M/F)

MEANING: "searching out"

SIGNIFICANCE: In the Bible, Tiria was a descendent of Judah, a son of Jacob.

KEY VERSE: Those who know your name trust in you, for you, O LORD, do not abandon those who search for you. (Ps. 9:10 NLT)

Tirzah (M/F)

MEANING: "benevolent"

SIGNIFICANCE: Tirzah was a town in the Promised Land, captured by Joshua, given to the tribe of Manasseh.

KEY VERSE: Live in harmony with one another; be sympathetic, love as brothers, be compassionate and humble. (1 Peter 3:8)

Tito (SEE ANDREW)

Tobal (SEE CHRISTOPHER)

Todd (M)

MEANING: "fox"

SIGNIFICANCE: Robert Todd Lincoln (1843–1926), son of Abraham and Mary Lincoln, became a lawyer and served as secretary of war and minister to Great Britain.

KEY VERSE: Your righteousness is like the mighty mountains, your justice like the ocean depths. You care for people and animals alike, O LORD. (Ps. 36:6 NLT)

Tola (M/F)

MEANING: "scarlet"

SIGNIFICANCE: In the Bible, Tola was a son of Issachar, a son of Jacob.

KEY VERSE: God's Word is better than a diamond, better than a diamond set between emeralds. You'll like it better than strawberries in spring, better than red, ripe strawberries. (Ps. 19:10 MSG)

Toman (SEE THOMAS)

Tomaz (SEE THOMAS)

Toncho (SEE ANTHONY)

Tonico (SEE ANTHONY)

T

Tonio (SEE ANTHONY)

Tora (SEE VICTORIA)

Torrey (M/F)

MEANING: "triumphant"

SIGNIFICANCE: R. A. Torrey (1856–1928) was an American evangelist, pastor, writer, and educator. At D. L. Moody's request he headed what was later called Moody Bible Institute.

KEY VERSE: For You, LORD, have made me glad through Your work; I will triumph in the works of Your hands. (Ps. 92:4 NKJV)

Tova (M/F)

MEANING: "goodly"

SIGNIFICANCE: Saint Tova (died 870) was a hermit and martyr.

KEY VERSE: Trust in the LORD and do good. Then you will live safely in the land and prosper. (Ps. 37:3 NLT)

Tovano (SEE VICTOR)

Tracie, Tracy (SEE ANASTASIA)

Trason (M/F)

MEANING: unknown

SIGNIFICANCE: Saint Trason (died 302) was

martyred during the persecutions of Diocletian for helping Christian prisoners.

KEY VERSE: The LORD is my strength and shield. I trust him with all my heart. He helps me, and my heart is filled with joy. I burst out in songs of thanksgiving. (Ps. 28:7 NLT)

Tressan (M/F)

MEANING: "harvester"

SIGNIFICANCE: Saint Tressan of Mareuil (died 550) was one of eight siblings who evangelized an area of France during the sixth century.

KEY VERSE: Peacemakers who sow in peace raise a harvest of righteousness. (James 3:18)

Trixie, Trixy (SEE BEATRICE)

Troyen (M)

MEANING: "descendent of the foot soldier"

SIGNIFICANCE: Saint Troyen (died 533) came to faith as an adult and served as the beloved bishop of Saintes, France.

KEY VERSE: With your help I can advance against a troop, with my God I can scale a wall. (Ps. 18:29)

Tudy (F)

MEANING: "divine gift" (from "Tudor")

SIGNIFICANCE: Saint Tudy (fifth century)

dedicated her life wholly to God, and has a church in Wales named for her.

KEY VERSE: Every good and perfect gift is from above, coming down from the Father of the heavenly lights, who does not change like shifting shadows. (James 1:17)

Turien (M/F)

MEANING: "privileged birth"

SIGNIFICANCE: Saint Turien (died c. 750) was a bishop in Brittany.

KEY VERSE: All praise to God, the Father of our Lord Jesus Christ. It is by his great mercy that we have been born again. (1 Peter 1:3 NLT)

Tyrrell (M)

MEANING: "thunder ruler"

SIGNIFICANCE: George Tyrrell (1861–1909) was a Roman Catholic priest and scholar who attempted to merge historic Catholic teaching with modern knowledge while maintaining religious authenticity and scholarly integrity.

KEY VERSE: The LORD thunders at the head of his army; his forces are beyond number, and mighty are those who obey his command. (Joel 2:11)

U

U

Ulric (M)

MEANING: "wolf powerful"

SIGNIFICANCE: Saint Ulric (890–973) built churches, visited parishioners, and ministered to the sick. His godly example resulted in improved moral and social conditions for all.

KEY VERSE: The wild animals honor me, the jackals and the owls, because I provide water in the desert and streams in the wasteland, to give drink to my people, my chosen. (Isa. 43:20)

Ulysses (M)

MEANING: "guide"

SIGNIFICANCE: Ulysses (Odysseus) is the main character in Homer's *Odyssey* and best known for being clever and resourceful in his adventures on his ten-year journey home after the Trojan War.

KEY VERSE: Since you are my rock and my fortress, for the sake of your name lead and guide me. (Ps. 31:3)

Urban (M)

MEANING: "town"

SIGNIFICANCE: Pope Urban VII (1521–90) experienced the shortest papal reign in history: thirteen days. He instituted the first known public smoking ban, threatening to excommunicate anyone who used tobacco on church property.

KEY VERSE: I'm thanking you, GOD, out loud in the streets, singing your praises in town and country. The deeper your love, the higher it goes; every cloud is a flag to your faithfulness. (Ps. 57:9 MSG)

Ursula (F)

MEANING: "bear"

U

SIGNIFICANCE: When she refused to deny her faith, Saint Ursula, a legendary princess, was martyred along with her companions.

KEY VERSE: [God] made all the stars—the Bear and Orion, the Pleiades and the constellations of the southern sky. He does great things too marvelous to understand. (Job 9:9–10 NLT)

Ussher (M)

MEANING: "river mouth"

SIGNIFICANCE: James Ussher (1581–1656) was an Irish archbishop famous for his Bible chronology, still found in the margins of some Bibles. Though now largely discredited, his calculations put the actual moment of creation at 9:00 a.m. on October 23, 4004 BC.

KEY VERSE: How precious is your unfailing love, O God! All humanity finds shelter in the shadow of your wings. You feed them from the abundance of your own house, letting them drink from your river of delights. (Ps. 36:7–8 NLT)

V

"REMEMBER THAT A MAN'S
NAME IS, TO HIM, THE
SWEETEST AND MOST
IMPORTANT SOUND IN ANY
LANGUAGE."

— DALE CARNEGIE

V

Vaise (M/F)

MEANING: "going"

SIGNIFICANCE: Saint Vaise (died c. 500) was a wealthy citizen who was put in jail and later martyred for giving his property to the poor.

KEY VERSE: God ... you keep me going when times are tough—my bedrock, GOD, since my childhood. I've hung on you from the day of my birth, the day you took me from the cradle; I'll never run out of praise. (Ps. 71:4–6 MSG)

Valentine (M/F)

MEANING: "strong"; "vigorous"

SIGNIFICANCE: Saint Valentine (died 269) was a physician and priest in Rome. He was jailed for helping prisoners, and while he was there, the jailer came to faith when Valentine restored the sight of the man's daughter.

KEY VERSE: Wait on the LORD; be of good courage, and He shall strengthen your heart; wait, I say, on the LORD! (Ps. 27:14 NKJV)

Valeria (F)

MEANING: "strong"

SIGNIFICANCE: Legendary Saint Valeria of Milan was martyred for giving decent burials to Christian martyrs and then refusing to sacrifice to pagan gods.

V

KEY VERSE: GOD makes his people strong. GOD gives his people peace. (Ps. 29:11 MSG)

Valiant (SEE VALENTINE)

Valida (SEE VALENTINE)

Vance (M)

MEANING: "very high places"

SIGNIFICANCE: Billy Graham once called Dr. Vance Havner (1901–86) the "Dean of America's Revival Preachers." His sense of humor and ability to phrase a thought so effectively as to make it unforgettable endeared him to many. When asked about the duties of a minister, Havner replied, "The preacher is to comfort the afflicted and afflict the comfortable."

> KEY VERSE: Your righteousness, O God, is very high, You who have done great things; O God, who is like You? (Ps. 71:19 NKJV)

Vando (M)

MEANING: "wanderer"

SIGNIFICANCE: Saint Vando (died c. 756) was a Benedictine monk and abbot of Fontenelle, France.

KEY VERSE: Make sure you stay alert. keep close watch over yourselves. Don't forget anything of what

V

you've seen. Don't let your heart wander off. Stay vigilant as long as you live. (Deut. 4:9 MSG)

Vaniah (F)

MEANING: "nourishment, or weapons, of the Lord"

SIGNIFICANCE: Vaniah's name appears in the book of Ezra in the Bible.

KEY VERSE: Let your roots grow down into him, and let your lives be built on him. Then your faith will grow strong in the truth you were taught, and you will overflow with thankfulness. (Col. 2:7 NLT)

Varelde (M/F)

MEANING: unknown

SIGNIFICANCE: Legend says that Saint Varelde (c. 650–740) caused a well to spring up whose waters cured sick children.

KEY VERSE: O LORD my God, I called to you for help and you healed me. (Ps. 30:2)

Varina (SEE BARBARA)

Vaughan (M)

MEANING: "little"

SIGNIFICANCE: Charles John Vaughan (1816–97) was a Welsh minister and scholar, known for the number of young men he trained for ordination.

V

KEY VERSE: The one who knows much says little; an understanding person remains calm. (Prov. 17:27 MSG)

Verena (F)

MEANING: "true"

SIGNIFICANCE: Saint Verena was known for caring for the poor and the sick, especially lepers.

KEY VERSE: Train me, GOD, to walk straight; then I'll follow your true path. Put me together, one heart and mind; then, undivided, I'll worship in joyful fear. (Ps. 86:11 MSG)

Veridiana (F)

MEANING: "fresh and young"

SIGNIFICANCE: According to legend, when famine struck her hometown, Saint Veridiana (1182–1242) gave away some beans to the poor. The next day the storage bins were mysteriously refilled.

KEY VERSE: Don't let anyone think less of you because you are young. Be an example to all believers in what you say, in the way you live, in your love, your faith, and your purity. (1 Tim. 4:12 NLT)

Veronica (F)

MEANING: "true image"

SIGNIFICANCE: According to legend, a woman

named Veronica wiped Jesus' face with a cloth as he walked toward Calvary. The image of his face remained on the towel, and the relic has become her symbol.

KEY VERSE: God created human beings in his own image. In the image of God he created them; male and female he created them. (Gen. 1:27 NLT)

Victor (M)

MEANING: "conqueror"

SIGNIFICANCE: Roman soldier Saint Victor (died c. 303), a Christian from his youth, lived his life in quiet praise to God. Despite this, he was arrested and martyred for his faith during the persecutions of Emperor Maximian.

KEY VERSE: Don't let evil conquer you, but conquer evil by doing good. (Rom. 12:21 NLT)

Victoria (F)

MEANING: "victory"

SIGNIFICANCE: Great Britain's Queen Victoria (1819–1901) reigned sixty-three years, longer than any other British monarch. Her reign resulted in the massive expansion of the British Empire and established it as a formidable global power. Incidentally, she is credited with starting the tradition of brides wearing white dresses on their wedding day.

KEY VERSE: Everyone runs; one wins. Run to win. (1 Cor. 9:24 MSG)

Vida (SEE DAVID)

Vincent (M)

MEANING: "prevailing"

SIGNIFICANCE: Saint Vincent de Paul (1581–1660) was taken captive by Turkish pirates and sold into slavery. Upon his owner's conversion he was released and returned to France where he founded organizations to help the poor, feed the hungry, and nurse the sick.

KEY VERSE: Everyone runs; one wins. Run to win. (1 Cor. 9:24 MSG)

Viret (M/F)

MEANING: "to be green"

SIGNIFICANCE: Pierre Viret (1511–71), an active Reformer and close associate to John Calvin, was considered in France to be the most popular French-speaking preacher in the sixteenth century.

KEY VERSE: I'm an olive tree, growing green in God's house. I trusted in the generous mercy of God then and now. (Ps. 52:8 MSG)

Virgil (M)

MEANING: "staff bearer"

SIGNIFICANCE: Saint Virgil (died 784) was a

Benedictine monk who was twice accused of heresy for his scientific ideas—including a round earth. He was cleared of the charges and went on to rebuild the Cathedral of Salzburg.

KEY VERSE: I will not be afraid, for you are close beside me. Your rod and your staff protect and comfort me. (Ps. 23:4 NLT)

Vito (SEE VICTOR)

Viviana (F)

MEANING: "lively"

SIGNIFICANCE: After their parents were martyred, Saint Viviana (died c. 361) and her sister were given to a woman who tried to force Viviana into prostitution. Upon her continued refusal, the woman had Viviana imprisoned and then killed.

KEY VERSE: As obedient children, let yourselves be pulled into a way of life shaped by God's life, a life energetic and blazing with holiness. (1 Peter 1:13 MSG)

W

"REMEMBER THAT A MAN'S NAME IS, TO HIM, THE SWEETEST AND MOST IMPORTANT SOUND IN ANY LANGUAGE."

— DALE CARNEGIE

W

Walden (M)

MEANING: "wooded valley"

SIGNIFICANCE: Though Saint Walden (c. 1100–1160) was born to English nobility, he chose a religious life and is remembered for his austere lifestyle and unfailing kindness to the poor.

KEY VERSE: The meadows are clothed with flocks of sheep, and the valleys are carpeted with grain. They all shout and sing for joy! (Ps. 65:13 NLT)

Waldo (M)

MEANING: "ruler"

SIGNIFICANCE: Peter Waldo (1150–1218) experienced a radical conversion and became passionate about spreading the truth of the Bible to anyone who would listen. His followers were known as Waldensians, and, lacking formal training in preaching, traveled the land simply quoting memorized portions of Scripture. They were severely persecuted but never gave up spreading God's Word in the language of the people to whom they ministered.

KEY VERSE: The Right and Justice are the roots of your rule; Love and Truth are its fruits. Blessed are the people who know the passwords of praise, who shout on parade in the bright presence of GOD. (Ps. 89:14–15 MSG)

W

Wallace (M)

MEANING: "stranger"

SIGNIFICANCE: Sir William Wallace (1270–1305) was a Scottish knight who led a resistance to the English occupation of Scotland. Little accurate information exists, but Wallace's legend lives on through several novels and films.

KEY VERSE: Do not forget to entertain strangers, for by so doing some people have entertained angels without knowing it. (Heb. 13:2)

Wendelin (M/F)

MEANING: "wander"

SIGNIFICANCE: Saint Wendelin (554–617) was a prince of Scotland who abandoned his life in the royal family and devoted himself to God.

KEY VERSE: With all my heart I have sought You; do not let me wander from Your commandments. (Ps. 119:10 NASB)

Wesley (M)

MEANING: "west meadow"

SIGNIFICANCE: John Wesley (1703–90) is the founder of Methodism. His focus on evangelism and holiness transformed the church and society in England. John's brother Charles is well known as a hymn writer, having penned "Hark, the Herald Angels Sing" among many others.

KEY VERSE: GOD, my shepherd! I don't need a thing. You have bedded me down in lush meadows, you find me quiet pools to drink from. True to your word, you let me catch my breath and send me in the right direction. (Ps. 23:1–3 MSG)

William (M)

MEANING: "determined guardian"

SIGNIFICANCE: William Wilberforce (1759–1833) almost single-handedly brought an end to slavery in the British Empire.

KEY VERSE: He won't let you stumble, your Guardian God won't fall asleep. (Ps. 121:3 MSG)

Winnoc (M/F)

MEANING: "little fair one"

SIGNIFICANCE: Though of noble birth, Saint Winnoc (died c. 716) founded the church, hospital, and monastery—of which he became abbot—of Wormhout near Dunkirk. He was known for his humility and willingness to work at any task in the monastery, no matter how difficult or disagreeable.

KEY VERSE: See that you do not look down on one of these little ones. For I tell you that their

$\mathcal{W}$

angels in heaven always see the face of my Father in heaven. (Matt. 18:10)

Wynnia (F)

MEANING: "blessed"

SIGNIFICANCE: Saint Wynnia was a sixth-century bishop who founded the monastery of Holywood.

KEY VERSE: You're blessed when you stay on course, walking steadily on the road revealed by GOD. You're blessed when you follow his directions, doing your best to find him. (Ps. 119:1 MSG)

Wystan (M)

MEANING: "battle stone"

SIGNIFICANCE: Saint Wystam of Evesham (died 849) was killed as a young man for defending his mother against an unworthy suitor.

KEY VERSE: Praise the LORD, who is my rock. He trains my hands for war and gives my fingers skill for battle. (Ps. 144:1 NLT)

"REMEMBER THAT A MAN'S NAME IS, TO HIM, THE SWEETEST AND MOST IMPORTANT SOUND IN ANY LANGUAGE."

— DALE CARNEGIE

X

Xico (M)

MEANING: "great field"

SIGNIFICANCE: Saint Thomas Xico (died 1597) was a pharmacist with a violent temper. Prayer and faith eventually brought it under control, and he became a Franciscan layperson. When the Franciscans opened a nearby convent, Thomas moved his pharmacy next door to it.

KEY VERSE: Let the fields and their crops burst fooutrth with joy! Let the trees of the forest rustle with praise before the LORD! (Ps. 96:12–13 NLT)

Ximon (SEE SIMON)

"REMEMBER THAT A MAN'S NAME IS, TO
HIM, THE SWEETEST AND MOST IMPORTANT
SOUND IN ANY LANGUAGE."

— DALE CARNEGIE

Y

Yalon (SEE JALON)

Yared (SEE JARED)

Yolanda (F)

MEANING: "violet flower"

SIGNIFICANCE: Saint Yolanda (died 1298) was a princess—her father was King Bela IV of Hungary—who entered the Poor Clares when her husband died and later became abbess at Gneson.

KEY VERSE: If God cares so wonderfully for wildflowers that are here today and thrown into the fire tomorrow, he will certainly care for you. (Matt. 6:30 NLT)

Z

"REMEMBER THAT A MAN'S
NAME IS, TO HIM, THE
SWEETEST AND MOST
IMPORTANT SOUND IN ANY
LANGUAGE."

— DALE CARNEGIE

Z

Zachary (M)

MEANING: "Jehovah remembers"

SIGNIFICANCE: Pope Zachary (died 752) was considered a wise and subtle diplomat, and his surviving correspondence with Saint Boniface of Germany shows his extensive influence over European politics of that time.

KEY VERSE: [God] has made His wonderful works to be remembered; the LORD is gracious and full of compassion. (Ps. 111:4 NKJV)

Zafra (M/F)

MEANING: "harvest"

SIGNIFICANCE: Saint John de Zafra (died 1570) was a Jesuit missionary martyr.

KEY VERSE: The LORD will indeed give what is good, and our land will yield its harvest. (Ps. 85:12)

Zaida (F)

MEANING: "prosperous"

SIGNIFICANCE: Saint Zaida (died c. 1180) was brought to faith by her brother Saint Bernard. Zaida and her brother and sister tried to convert their brother Almanzor, who turned them over to the authorities. All three were eventually martyred.

KEY VERSE: Trust in the LORD and do good. Then you will live safely in the land and prosper. (Ps. 37:3 NLT)

Z

Zarah (SEE SARAH)

Zebulun (M)

MEANING: "honor"

SIGNIFICANCE: In the Bible, Zebulun was a son of Jacob and Leah.

KEY VERSE: My victory and honor come from God alone. He is my refuge, a rock where no enemy can reach me. (Ps. 62:7 NLT)

Zechariah (M)

MEANING: "the Lord remembers"

SIGNIFICANCE: In the Bible, Zechariah was the father of John the Baptist, the prophet who prepared the way for the Messiah.

KEY VERSE: The LORD remembers us and will bless us. (Ps. 115:12 NLT)

Zeno (M)

MEANING: "sign"

SIGNIFICANCE: Saint Zeno (died 249) was a Roman soldier who guarded a group of Egyptian Christians. During their trial, he encouraged them not to abandon their faith. Later arrested as a Christian, he was martyred.

KEY VERSE: Mark me with your sign of love. Plan only the best for me, GOD! (Ps. 25:7 MSG)

Z

Zia (F)

MEANING: "grain"

SIGNIFICANCE: In the Bible, Zia was a clan leader of the tribe of Gad.

KEY VERSE: You take care of the earth and water it, making it rich and fertile. The river of God has plenty of water; it provides a bountiful harvest of grain, for you have ordered it so. (Ps. 65:9 NLT)

Zillah (F)

MEANING: "shadow"

SIGNIFICANCE: In the Bible, Zillah was a wife of a descendent of Enoch, the man whom the Bible says "walked with God" (Gen. 5:24).

KEY VERSE: Those who live in the shelter of the Most High will find rest in the shadow of the Almighty. (Ps. 91:1 NLT)

Zita (F)

MEANING: "seeker"

SIGNIFICANCE: Saint Zita (1218–72) became a domestic servant at age twelve and remained in that position her whole life. She often gave her food, and that of her master, to the poor.

KEY VERSE: My heart says of you, "Seek his face!" Your face, LORD, I will seek. (Ps. 27:8)

Ziza (M)

MEANING: "splendor"; "abundance"

SIGNIFICANCE: In the Bible, Ziza was a chief in the tribe of Simeon.

KEY VERSE: GOD made the heavens—royal splendor radiates from him, a powerful beauty sets him apart. (Ps. 96:5 MSG)

Zoe (F)

MEANING: "life"

SIGNIFICANCE: Saint Zoe of Rome (died c. 286) was married to a high court official in imperial Rome. One day during the persecutions of Emperor Diocletian, she was arrested for her faith while praying at the tomb of the apostle Peter. She was later martyred.

KEY VERSE: You [God] will show me the way of life, granting me the joy of your presence and the pleasures of living with you forever. (Ps. 16:11 NLT)

Zola (F)

MEANING: "quietness"

SIGNIFICANCE: Saint John Baptist Zola (1576–1626) was a Jesuit missionary to both India and Japan.

KEY VERSE: In quietness and confidence is your strength. (Isa. 30:15 NLT)

Zubin (SEE ZEBULON)

Sources

BOOKS

Comfort, Philip, and Walter A. Elwell. *The Complete Book of Who's Who in the Bible.* Wheaton, IL: Tyndale, 2004.

Diamant, Anita. *Bible Baby Names.* Woodstock, VT: Jewish Lights, 1996.

Garlow, James L. *God and His People.* Colorado Springs: Victor, 2004.

Hudson, Robert R., and Shelley Townsend-Hudson. *Companions for the Soul.* Grand Rapids: Zondervan, 1995.

Lansky, Bruce. *The Best Baby Name Book in the Whole Wide World.* Deephaven, MN: Meadowbrook, 1984.

Modica, Terry A. *Daily Prayers with the Saints for the New Millennium.* Good News Ministries Online: www.gnm.org: 1998.

Merriam-Webster's Collegiate Dictionary (11th ed.). Springfield, MA: Merriam-Webster, Incorporated, 2004.

WEB SITES

http://babiesonline.com/babynames, accessed 7/8/06.

http://babyfit.com/baby-names.asp, accessed 7/15/06.

http://britannia.com/history/h12.html, accessed 7/14/06.

http://chi.gospelcom.net/morestories/jamestown.shtml, accessed 8/28/06.

http://einmal-ist-keinmal.blogspot.com/2006/07/so-ive-been-visiting-ccf-very-often.html, accessed 8/13/06.

http://elbalero.gob.mx/kids/explora/html/queretaro/index.html, accessed 7/15/06.

http://italian.about.com/library/name/blname_macaria.htm, accessed 8/13/06.

http://literature.all-about-switzerland.info/johanna-spyri-heidi-girl-alps.html, accessed 8/22/06.

http://pregnancy.parenthood.com/babynames.html, accessed 7/10/06.

http://thesixbells.blogspot.com/2004/07/carmelite-martyrs-of-compiegne-on-this.html, accessed 8/13/06.

http://vancehavner.org, accessed 7/15/06.

http://wordbytes.org/saints/names-girls-ab.htm, accessed 8/12/06.

http://www.20000-names.com/index.htm, accessed 8/11/06.

http://www.800florals.com/care/meaning.asp, accessed 8/25/06.

http://www.actapublications.com/names.html, accessed 7/25/06.

http://www.babynameaddicts.com/, accessed 8/14/06.

http://www.babynamesworld.com, accessed 3/17/06.

http://www.behindthename.com/nm/a.html, accessed 9/12/05.

http://www.catholic-forum.com/Saints/patron02.htm, accessed 4/1/06.

http://www.catholicpilgrims.com, accessed 8/5/06.

http://www.christiananswers.net//dictionary/home.html, accessed 6/30/06.

http://www.christianitytoday.com/history/features/131christians.html, accessed 5/15/06.

http://www.daire.org/names/celtcornmale.html, accessed 7/14/06.

http://www.earlybritishkingdoms.com/bios/teilo.html, accessed 8/28/06.

http://www.gemstone.org, accessed 7/2/06.

http://www.my-baby-names.com, accessed 7/2/06.

http://www.sacred-texts.com/neu/celt/cg2/cg2107.htm, accessed 7/25/06.

http://www.saintpatrickdc.org/ss/0903.htm, accessed 7/30/06.

http://www.scottish.parliament.uk/vli/language/gaelic/pdfs/placenamesA-B.pdf, accessed 7/25/06.

http://www.thinkbabynames.com, accessed 6/4/06.

http://www.umilta.net/hildegard.html, accessed 7/25/06.

http://www.usarchery.org/usarchery/html/History.html, accessed 7/4/06.

http://www.wtu.edu/franciscan/pages/groups/clares/index.html, accessed 5/12/06.

Additional copies of this and other Honor
are available wherever good books are sold.

If you have enjoyed this book, or if it has had an impact on your life,
we would like to hear from you.

Please contact us at:

HONOR BOOKS
Cook Communications Ministries, Dept. 240
4050 Lee Vance View
Colorado Springs, CO 80918

Or visit our Web site
www.cookministries.com

HONOR HB BOOKS

Inspiration and Motivation for the Seasons of Life